Planning and Organizing Group Activities in Social Recreation

Planning and Organizing Group Activities in Social Recreation

by John V. Valentine

Venture Publishing, Inc.
State College, Pennsylvania

Production Manager: Richard Yocum
Manuscript Editing: Valerie Fowler, Richard Yocum, Michele L. Barbin
Illustrations by Gail Fusco
Cover by Echelon Design

Library of Congress Catalogue Card Number 2005938308
ISBN-10 1-892132-61-3
ISBN-13 978-1-892132-61-1

Dedications

To my one and only son, David Ian, who has always inspired me to work hard and to continue to improve myself. He is a true companion, who knows me so very well, and knows that his mother and I love him more than anything else in the world. We want him to know how much we are grateful to share this period of time with him. Without him this book would probably never have been completed.

To my wife, Eileen, who with her talent, sagacious deportment, and moral fortitude has always urged me on to do the "right thing." In this case, it was to complete this book. Thank you for your patience and tolerance in allowing me the time to work on this book.

To my instructors—Dr. Ken Benson, now a retired professor from Kean University, and Robert Marashlian, a retired teacher from Elizabeth High School—who taught me many of these activities.

To Fred Marder, a superb instructor, a fine friend, and a very kind gentleman, who consistently guided me in the right direction when I was not sure which path to take.

To the many students who have contributed to my knowledge base and who have demonstrated to me the importance of being tolerant and patient and who always point out to me the difference between what is successful and what is not successful.

Acknowledgments

Of enormous value to this book is the cooperation and assistance given by Richard Yocum at Venture Publishing. His willingness to see it completed, his clarity in outlining the details of the appearance of the book, and the precise manner in which he undertook the coordination between the requirements of the printer and the assumed notions I had prior to editing were of utmost value. I am indeed most grateful for his kind willingness to see this project to the end.

I am deeply grateful to my wife, Eileen, for assisting me with proofreading when she was very tired from her own work as music director and graduate student.

Many thanks to Dr. Kenneth Benson and to the late William Lavery, who always encouraged me to write this book.

Table of Contents

Preface

This book is intended for recreation leaders working in community recreation settings, high school teachers, professors who teach physical education and/or recreation courses, camp counselors, or any coordinators, directors, and group leaders interested in expanding their repertoire of social recreation activities and concerned with developing a memorable, positive experience among the group with whom they work.

The approach to this book is to share the most successful activities one might encounter when planning, organizing, and leading activities and recreation programs. The activities selected are those that do not require excessive experience in recreation activity leadership or presenting fun activities to groups of people. Instead of including the largest number of activities that could be found, the activities selected are those most promising for instant success.

This book allows facilitators to plan a social recreation program with the greatest ease. Each activity includes the category to which it belongs (recognizing, of course, that some activities can be modified to fit into more than one category). These categories place activities into four basic areas: instruction, demonstration/entertainment, competition, or free play. The purpose of the categories is to allow the leader to set up a program of activities with a variety of activities (e.g., not having a game session with just competitive games that breed discontent and only turn participants into winners and losers).

This approach to recreation fun sessions is very much needed in today's society, as competition (in sports, in particular) has led to many disgruntled players and discontented participants who would much rather have a relaxed, casual experience not marked by commercialized and impersonal forms of recreation. Instead, the activities selected here promote cooperative and constructive forms of leisure utilizing supportive and positive relationships among participants.

The margins on most of the pages are increased to allow space for making notes.

Chapter One
Introduction

Due to a substantial increase in discretionary spending and disposable time since World War II, Americans have seen the growth of the recreation and leisure profession. For most people in the United States, during this modern "age-of-information," the recognition of the importance of recreation and leisure has grown markedly. Since the late 1940s there has been an increase in holidays, vacations, and retirements, along with the recognition of the leisure needs of special populations (e.g., persons with social, mental, and physical disabilities). Leisure today presents us with a vast number of opportunities. For the majority, it represents freedom—a chance to do what one chooses without the constraints of work obligations.

American society was built on the Puritan (or Protestant) work ethic. This ethic proposed that good work done here on earth would ensure a place in heaven, and that continuous labor for the glory of God was our chief purpose here on earth. The Puritan work ethic has given us respect for hard work and has paved the way for our current mode of thinking and behaving; however, it has also left residual scars on a society that questions the value of leisure time. In modern society this view is now being challenged. The work ethic came under severe scrutiny during the 1960s when America developed new concerns for political and economic security, which resulted in a movement for social change. Since that time reports have indicated that many middle-age citizens are not content with their lifestyles and do not know what to do with their leisure time (Allen & Beattie, 1984; Diener, 2000; Frank, 1999; Jackson, 1990; Kay & Jackson, 1991; Myers & Diener, 1997; Nelson, 2000; Tangley, 2000; Yankelovich, 1982).

From colonial times through the industrial revolution, the work projects of our forebears were enough to bring them close together and to feel a sense of belonging and purpose. Today, many jobs are done sitting alone at a desk with no sustained group effort to complete a task. Most workers today complain of "job stress" and have developed defensive shells, while multitudinous workaholics abound. Numerous individuals seek to satisfy their leisure needs by traveling to distant resorts or to find a haven "where everybody knows your name." Many do not recognize, nor were they given the orientation to explore at earlier ages, what will satisfy their leisure needs.

In some cases, young persons become attracted to groups who do not hold customs and traditional moral practices in high regard, and the consequences of this for our modern society can be devastating. Fortunately, there are several organizations that recognize the needs of youth today, and are moving in the direction of affording teenagers and young adults places to go and activities to do that keep with wholesome and healthy lifestyles.

In these modern times, a marked change in leisure behavior of past generations has caused us to rethink the efforts we should be putting toward recreation and to carefully consider its potential in reducing many of the social issues that confront us. At the start of the 20th century, social institutions (e.g., the church, family) had much influence in establishing roles for individuals. A little over 100 years later, we have witnessed a decline in the influence of these social institutions. In particular, the growth of educating masses and changes in the attitudes of people toward leisure behaviors, including tolerance and the acceptance of diversity and multiculturalism built around the development of a heterogeneous society, has afforded North Americans to indulge in the widest variety of recreation pursuits in the world. We are now faced with an enormous number of recreation activities from which to choose. For many individuals the pursuit of pleasure as an end in itself has become one choice. There appears to be an emphasis on a hedonistic, thrill-seeking way of life, which often includes risk-taking adventures, gambling, alcohol, or drugs. For so many young people today, there seems to be an ongoing search for excitement and challenge. Included in this are the video games that depict and may even encourage violence, killing, and destruction. Other examples of this are activities, such as hang-gliding, skydiving, motorcycle hill climbing, or riding speeding roller coasters. This book attempts to teach alternatives to these sensation-seeking activities and to demonstrate that there is a real benefit to participating in activities that allow for personal expression in group settings and encourage group acceptance.

The Age of Information

Individuals today face an extraordinary amount of information at a very rapid speed, which is unprecedented in the history of mankind. To support the point that our modern society has made significant changes in lifestyles and behaviors, consider the way in which information has been passed along throughout history. Information flow doubled in the 1,500 years between the time of Jesus and Leonardo DaVinci. It doubled again by the year 1750 (i.e., in about 250 years). The next doubling only took about 150 years to the turn of the century. The onset of the computer age reduced the doubling time to about five years. The amount of information to which the average individual is now exposed doubles every year.

Consciously, however, we can only process about seven (plus or minus two) chunks of information before it is lost. Read the following list of numbers, stare at them for one minute, close the book briefly, and then try to write them all down:

6   38   57   19   121   83   41   917   64   817   24

Undoubtedly, most readers will have only been able to write up to half of the numbers. Our minds are indeed limited as to how much information we can retain. Much of this sort of "information overload" is a creator of distress.

Distress: The Role of Stress in Modern Society

Modern-day stress is a common fact of life in most U.S. urban and suburban communities. These stressors demand adaptations to myriad changes that face many families today—divorce, separation, single-parent families, job changes, moving, personal loss, problems concerning money—and can result in extreme cases of anxiety and depression. While many of us experience some natural anxiety and a certain amount of depression, prolonged tension levels can escalate into serious problems. As many readers of this book know, health issues such as high blood pressure, migraine headaches, and the inability to enjoy life can result from the unrelenting and unresolved challenges of modern lifestyles. Knowing about the factors that affect stress levels can do a lot to keep tensions within reasonable limits before they lead to trouble. While social recreation has many benefits in terms of what it can offer individuals in regard to physical, emotional, social, and cognitive well-being, it certainly cannot be considered a cure-all for managing stress. However, if given the opportunity, social recreation does provide outstanding practical potential that can assist people to gain a fuller, contented, and happier spirit of group participation. Social recreation can be an excellent way to find new forms of self-renewal in leisure activities, in addition to improving and strengthening community life and contributing to physical and mental health.

Recreation Pastimes Today

As an example of the current state of recreation and leisure pastimes, many college students appear to lack the necessary knowledge and skills to conduct recreation activities that are not sports or athletics. For them, recreation has simply meant sports and athletics. They do not immediately recognize that recreation includes a multitude of other activities, including dramatics, arts, crafts, music, dance, games, and cultural and nature activities. These students are high school graduates from school systems that typically provide physical education and art as an orientation to leisure. More recently, however, many schools are beginning to recognize the need to satisfy students' interests beyond academics and the arts. Most often, these "progressive" schools offer alternatives to sports and art classes in the form of memberships to voluntary school clubs.

As a result of the decrease in physical fatigue associated with many forms of employment (i.e., the majority of employees today are not construction, mining, lumber, or farm workers), several issues have developed. One constructive outcome is the growing number of fitness centers and physically active pursuits. However, in addition, there has been widespread practice to use leisure time in pubs, bars, or saloons with the intention of satisfying the need for social contact. Yet another issue is the well-known fact that the most popular use of free time today is television watching. With the introduction of satellite dish and cable TV, the swell in time spent watching television has increased substantially. Watching TV has steadily increased since 1965, and accounts for over 18 hours of our free time per week on average (Godbey, 2003; McLean, Hurd & Rogers, 2005). A major concern, particularly among parents, is that TV has also become the common babysitter. Children may be encouraged to take a spectator-oriented approach to leisure rather than take a participatory role. If television watching and the related practice of playing video games consume children's lifestyles and time, children may not be given enough opportunity to explore their personal creative talents on their own, or ways in which they can be independent from artificial stimuli and activities that may distort their perception of reality. Before the age of television (approximately 60 years ago), individuals were self-reliant (i.e., in the search for talents and skills) to keep entertained; they would participate in group activities that included singing together, dancing, and exchanging stories, coincidences, and humorous experiences. Familial and friendship activities were common before the invention of television.

Creativity is a significant part of recreation and leisure. Individuals can be very creative during their leisure when feeling relaxed and engaging in brainstorming. Imaginative thinking or experimentation can be conducted with little regard for personal image or the pressures or constraints of continuous, productive output found in most employment. The sorts of things that block creativity often include the fear that one will fail. Often one is not creative simply because of lack of effort or knowledge. Certainly, creativity is held at bay when it comes to habit and conformity. In this modern world, there are too many individuals who are stuck with a routine of doing the same activities repeatedly. Recreation and leisure activities, and especially social recreation, allow individuals to express themselves in relaxed ways that can help to utilize their creativity.

The importance of students' leisure pastimes is increasingly being more carefully considered, and numerous studies have been conducted regarding the significance of social interaction and its influence on personal choices. While student voluntary clubs have been traditionally offered as a means of "getting involved," the inordinate number of students that have need for personal expression and the feeling of contributing and belonging to a group, far outnumber members of voluntary clubs. Far too few schools provide leisure education as part of the required curriculum. We should not assume that the traditional institutions (e.g., the family, temple) will provide the necessary outlets for leisure satisfaction. The conventional practice of the constructive use of leisure being taught in the home is nearly obsolete. With the growth of single-parent families, smaller family units, and increasing isolation, there is a growing need for opportunities with culturally enriching experiences for young adults who are not sports/athletics oriented.

This book will assist recreation directors or coordinators, teachers, students, and group workers in selecting and preparing activities that are not sports, gymnastics, athletics, or the fine arts. These activities are known in the recreation and leisure profession as social recreation activities. This book is designed to provide much needed information on leadership styles, techniques, and principles of group dynamics essential to all successful social recreation activities.

The information in this text can be effectively used as a guide and compendium of successful social recreation activities for adult groups. Although the social recreation activities included in this book are intended for adults, many of the games, dances, music activities, and skits can be adapted for use with teenagers and children ages eight and older.

Planning Events and Programs

Planning is the process of preparing for change and uncertainty by formulating future courses of action. Successful recreation programs for large numbers of people do not happen by chance. While spontaneity is a very important ingredient in defining "fun," truly successful activity programs and special events require careful planning and productive group dynamics. Having a sensible philosophy that takes into account the varied interests of individuals and accepts and understands individual differences is a very important component in the planning of activities. For the activity program to operate smoothly without hitches, the leader must be well-prepared and give careful thought to the set-up and the conclusion. Planning must include particular descriptions of intentions, processes, and expected outcomes.

While it is important to consider all factors that comprise the makeup of the group with which one is working, it is particularly worthy of note for planners of recreation programs to consider differences in the attitudes and behaviors between males and females. The notion of what constitutes fun is quite divided. Naturally, planners would want to ensure that there be maximum participation by both sexes. This participation can be enabled and strongly encouraged by carefully taking into account the actions that will be taken prior to, during, and at the close of each activity.

To meet the individual differences and various needs of participants when planning a program of social recreation activities, Maslow's Hierarchy of Human Needs should be considered. This hierarchy indicates that individuals must first have their *physiological needs* met (e.g., food, shelter, other basic needs), next *safety needs* should be satisfied (e.g., self-protection), *social needs* comprise the next level to be gratified, *ego needs* (e.g., enhanced status, self-esteem, confidence) must next be fulfilled, and finally one may reach his or her maximum potential and appease his or her need for creativity, this he labeled as *self-actualization.* Therefore, in planning a social recreation event, it is strongly recommended that the leader weigh each of these needs in regard to the preparation for the planned event. This will assist the leader in fulfilling the desired goals and may then contribute to self-actualization.

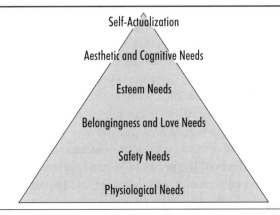

Participant Needs (based Upon Maslow's Hierarchy of Human Needs)

When this hierarchy has been considered, and the interests and desires of the group have been mindfully respected, the leader can confidently begin to organize the activities program.

Organizing

One factor that distinguishes this book is that the activities offered are those that have proven to be successful over many years and do not require extensive leadership ability. Organizing yourself as leader before your presentation is paramount. Indeed, participants can sense the amount of preparation that goes into a recreation program. Participants will almost immediately recognize poor planning and poor organization. A well-thought-out sequence of activities makes for a confident presentation.

In addition to having events occur in a logical sequence, have materials arranged in order. The rationale for this may be that the universe has order, and, this order descends to the very details of one's presentation. An essential element in organizing oneself is to ensure that clear directions have been well-thought-out before they are given—this reduces confusion and maintains group control. When organizing a recreation program, leaders must be conscience of the various age groups and their different approaches to leisure activities.

There is much fun, pleasure, and satisfaction derived from organizing. It appears to be a fundamental characteristic of all higher functioning animals. Once an individual has experienced the contentment resulting from organizing himself or herself, he or she will inevitably recognize the benefits of orderliness and attain the accompanying sense of fulfillment.

There are several approaches to organizing oneself for a presentation or program of activities. One such approach is simply to design the intended presentation or program on the basis of a previous observation. Once the intended presenter has determined that the activity or activities witnessed were of the quality appropriate for use in his or her own repertoire of activities, then he or she would organize the activities in the same fashion. In this case the presenter or leader would have evaluated the effects of the presentation and follow the procedures in the pattern as it was delivered in the past. Whatever the approach, the presenter or leader should arrange his or her presentation as an orderly process to enable him or her to predict the results of the actions to be taken. Another approach is one in which the organizer or presenter has a hunch that the selection of activities will meet the group's needs and interests. This is a very common approach, and one that can often achieve the intended goal. If the presenter has premeditated the order of events, has deliberated over the sequence of activities, and has taken calculated steps to ensure that the presentation makes sense to all participants, then there will be agreement among group members that the activity or activities were successful.

Definition and Purpose of Social Recreation

Social recreation is a type of leisure event. It is comprised of the familiar, casual, and enjoyable experiences conducted by a leader to promote relaxed and appropriate social behavior within groups. Fundamentally, social recreation activities could be almost any organized leisure event, conducted by a leader, which is not a sports, athletic, or artistic event. Typically, these activities are conducted indoors.

The primary intentions here are to have students (a) develop appropriate/respectful attitudes toward recreation and leisure and gain an appreciation, or retain their appreciation, for leisure activities with groups; (b) develop a repertoire of activities to lead; (c) become expressive, open, and sensitive to others; and (d) to develop social recreation leadership techniques.

Examples of Social Recreation Events

Social recreation can be found or conducted during many social events or gatherings. Examples of social recreation events include the following:

- company picnics
- award nights
- retirement dinners
- holiday parties
- birthday parties
- social gatherings
- student activities
- club meetings

Despite its seemingly freestyle approach, social recreation cannot be conducted just anywhere. It is most successful in settings that afford the leader control of the group and of the setting's arrangement. While nearly all social recreation events are more fun outdoors, it is more common to find groups meeting in rooms and large halls. Groups typically meet in restaurants, meeting halls, classrooms, catering facilities, and perhaps in someone's home. These settings are well-suited for social recreation activities. The minimum appropriate number of individuals for social recreation program activities is six.

Providers and Sponsors of Social Recreation

The following list constitutes the sponsors of social recreation programs:

- municipal recreation and park departments (e.g., in New Jersey each municipality has such a department)
- youth serving agencies (e.g., YMCAs, Boys & Girls Clubs, Scouts)
- religious organizations
- church and synagogue groups
- service organizations (e.g., Lions Club, Kiwanis Club, Masons)
- senior citizens clubs
- businesses or corporations
- education institutions (e.g., college/university campuses)
- armed forces (e.g., service clubs)

Today, a popular endeavor for employee clubs or associations is to sponsor sports leagues, charter vacation travel, stress-reduction programs, or hobby classes and clubs. Social recreation activities are well-suited for these types of programs as well as company picnics and holiday parties. Of course, social recreation is widely found in nonprofit agencies or organizations (e.g., Boys & Girls Clubs, Boy Scouts or Girl Scouts, YMCAs/YWCAs, and YMHAs/YWHAs). Many religious organizations of various types sponsor social recreation programs (e.g., church fellowship groups). Of particular interest are senior citizens' clubs, who find these types of activities stimulating and enjoyable. Educational groups on college and university campuses often sponsor such programs. Government agencies, including military personnel and their families, frequently provide social recreation programs. Under the government supported morale, welfare, and recreation (MWR) programs, social recreation is a well-accepted alternative to competitive sports events.

Places Where Social Recreation May Be Conducted

Because of the "personality" of social recreation activities it would appear that these fun activities can be conducted anywhere. This is not so. Social recreation, due to its format, requires strong leadership. While it may be true that social activities can ignite on their own, usually it takes a long time for that to occur. This is not the intention of social recreation. Because most groups that gather in a specified setting for a specified time period are quite eager to interact and want to feel their time is being spent wisely, they will react when such an opportunity is presented by an individual in a leadership position. Social recreation may often be found in the following settings:

- community centers
- restaurants
- chartered travel
- taverns or pubs
- meeting rooms
- banquet or catering halls
- picnic grounds
- health spas
- classrooms
- resorts

Classification of Social Recreation Events

Because of the great number of individual activities, it is helpful to have a system of classification of social recreation events. The following is a classification of social recreation activities (i.e., the categorical headings for social recreation):

- social or group games
- demonstration of tricks and puzzles
- musical activities
- dances
- dramatic activities
- craft and cooking demonstrations

Each of the classifications of social recreation listed here may be found among three levels of participation:

1. special events
2. program activities
3. clubs or groups that meet occasionally

In other words, an individual might participate on a rare occasion (e.g., special event), or participate on a regular, or daily, basis (e.g., program activities), or participate on an infrequent schedule, such as club members do.

Four Categories of Social Recreation

In addition to classifying social recreation activities, it is advanta
geous to understand that each activity can also be organized in
four different ways. All social recreation activities will fit into at
least one of the following four categories:

1. free play—activities that do not have a winner or
    winners; they may appear to go on without a given
    ending, thus requiring assertive leadership.

2. instruction—activities conducted in a classroom (e.g.,
    teaching a leisure hobby, a sport, or a crafts project).

3. competition—activities that have a winner (or winners),
    as do the majority of games.

4. demonstration or entertainment—activities such as an
    individual performance of a song, dance, or musical
    presentation.

Traits and Conceptualization

Social recreation is one format of the many different types of recreation program activities. Many of us are familiar with competitive programs, workshops, conferences, special interest groups,
open formats, or drop-in formats. Social recreation is yet another
type of format with certain characteristics that distinguish it from
other types.

Following are several reasons why social recreation is distinct:

*   The emphasis in social recreation is on the interrela-
    tionships of people. The participants attend or are involved
    primarily because they want to meet others or enjoy being
    with others.

*   While social recreation requires much planning and
    preparation by the leader, it demands little or no advance
    preparation on the part of the participant.

*   Unlike sports, athletics, and fine arts (including music
    and dance), the emphasis on degree of skill for perform-
    ers is minimized.

*   The emphasis is on cooperation, not competition.

*   The approach to the activities is usually informal. Lead-
    ers do not insist or command others to participate; instead
    they encourage potential members to participate at least
    three times.

- The event can take place almost anytime, anywhere, and with any number of people from four individuals to twenty-five.
- No special equipment is needed by the participant. Many items may be needed by the participant or leader; however, the tools of social recreation are varied.
- The event should be an integrating activity, if it is truly in the social recreation realm. It should give repeated opportunities for the participants to meet and mingle.

Goals and Objectives of Social Recreation

Social recreation intends to bring people together for relaxed sociability and friendly interchange in group settings. Unlike many other recreation formats—in which competition, winning, and personal gain are the chief motivators—the goals of social recreation are more varied and community oriented. They include the following:

- to provide cooperative and positive group relationships, including morale and cohesion
- to develop new and enhance old friendships
- to encourage the positive use of leisure time
- to expand ranges of interest in music, dance, drama, art, literature
- to develop leadership techniques
- to provide a means of fundraising for an agency or organization
- to provide opportunities for emotional release and relaxation
- to develop a sense of personal worth and enrichment of personality
- to identify with others and to experience the accompanying sense of belonging
- to provide for experiences in democratic living
- to allow for self-expression and creative experience

Examination of the Recreation Interests of Different Age Groups

One of the leading proponents of age group differences is Erik Erickson. While his work was quite detailed regarding the stages of life, the discussion here is to recognize that there are major differences and to merely point out some of the foremost distinctions between age groups as they pertain to social recreation.

At approximately age seven or eight, children begin to enter more formal recreation programs. They are drawn into organized groups and clubs, such as the Scouts or Boys and Girls Clubs, or little league sports. Younger children, whose ages are lower than seven, may experience planned activities in nursery schools or kindergartens or community playgrounds and often are taught simple games, engage in singing, or make crafts. While these play activities are indeed valuable, they are not truly social recreation as we will study the concept here. One important aspect of cooperative learning with children who are age seven or above, is the idea that they learn to become "good sports"—that is, they learn to recognize that it is okay, or acceptable, to not always win and that we cannot always be a winner.

For teenagers or adolescents, recreation and leisure are serious matters. This is a difficult period in the growth stage, for it is during this time that peer pressure is quite intense. It is during these years that individuals typically encounter tension between the values stated by their parents and those stated or practiced by their peers. For this age group, recreation is the time when they may demonstrate their skills, and aptitudes, or it might mean the distinct expression of attitudes conflicting with those of parents and society. Oftentimes there is tremendous pressure to engage in drinking, drugs, or sexual activity. The need to belong is very strong during this period of life and many times adolescents will engage in leisure pursuits simply to feel the approval of their friends. As a consequence, if the activities in which they engage are not considered appropriate, or contradict the norms of society, they consequently have a feeling of guilt or are confused about taking part in such activities. This often occurs as a result of not being certain of their own values or perhaps they are unaware of the alternative leisure activities that are available. For adolescents, well-organized social recreation activities can provide attractive and socially approved means of fun with their peers. As many youth-serving agencies have learned, one of the ways to encourage adolescents to partake in social recreation programs is to give them abundant support in designing and planning their own activity programs or special events. Indeed, many youth-serving agencies (e.g., Boys and Girls Clubs, Ys, Scouts, 4-H Clubs, religious organizations) face the challenge of providing activities that affirm positive social and moral values—leisure activities that emphasize the building of positive character traits and that are health-conscious. Recreation programs are challenged with providing alternatives to negative activities (e.g., drugs, sex, violence) and selecting activities that offer positive social and moral values.

Young adults (ages 19–29) are typically faced with having greater independence and often being on their own in the business world. Their recreation mainly consists of going to dances, singles bars, or activities of continuing social groups (e.g., meeting an informal group of friends each weekend at a local restaurant or bar).

Most middle-age adults (ages 30–59) usually carry on their recreation and leisure activities within their family units. Their recreation for the most part is with other couples and their families.

The majority of older adults (ages 60+) tends to withdraw from social situations and become isolated. This situation inevitably leads to loneliness coupled with psychological and physical deterioration. For many older adults, the concept of retirement is undesirable. Recreation can offer an alternative to this sort of psychological depression and can afford the elderly person a new approach to obtaining a new identity and new ways of reaching heightened self-esteem.

Chapter Two
Leadership in Social Recreation

A leader of social recreation program activities must be assertive and outgoing and speak with confidence in a loud, clear
voice. To not do so would mean that an awful lot of time would
be spent by a group searching for something meaningful to do.
A social recreation leader is one who directly leads and is continuously in touch with the participants by observing, encouraging, and interacting with them. In many situations, the role of
the social recreation leader is short-lived (for perhaps fifteen to
fifty minutes), therefore, the type of leadership required is quite
demanding. The social leader is not an entertainer, nor simply
a host. The successful social recreation leader has a true, deep
adoration for working with groups of people and demonstrates
a sense of purpose, direction, and enthusiasm that is evident
to all concerned. In addition, the good social recreation leader
should have an authentic sense of humor and be willing to be
flexible when everything does not go as planned.

Theories of Leadership

There are several theories as to why one becomes a leader.
Here, four major and pertinent theories of leadership will be
discussed. When asked what determines that someone in a
group will become a leader, often the response will be because
he or she automatically sees the solution or the pathway to re-
solve the issue or problem. The leadership theory that addresses
this is the *functional theory* of leadership. This theory indicates
that when an individual sees a way to handle the problem at
hand, he or she is very likely to become the leader of the group.

The theory of leadership that brings an individual to the
role of leader because he or she is in the right place at the right
time, or because the group chooses him or her, is the *situational
theory*. This theory says that a person becomes the leader of the
group if the circumstances are such that the individual selected
for leadership just happens to appear appropriate at the time
leadership is necessary.

Often a leader is one who represents the commonality of
the group. A theory historically recognized for leadership positions is *trait theory*. Simply put, an individual is accepted as

leader, as per this theory, because he or she is the "heir to the throne," perhaps because his or her family member, or members, have always had a leadership position. This theory indicates that this leader is endowed with certain qualities and has a special charisma for leadership (e.g., great figures in history, such as Alexander the Great and Napoleon).

The fourth theory of leadership that is applicable to our understanding of why one becomes a leader is *contingency theory*. This theory points out that an individual serves as a leader only because the group allows him or her to do so, and that certain factors must be in place for this individual to lead. The power ascribed to this leader is due to the nature of the task, its difficulty, and the leader's ability to assign the right kind of duties. For example, if the leader chooses a task that is too difficult or too simple, the group will quickly lose interest in following him or her.

Group Leadership Styles

Traditionally, since World War II, three styles of leadership have been discussed in relevant literature.

1. The *authoritarian* style represents an individual who has a dictatorial approach to leading. He or she is rather bossy and almost tyrannical in getting the job accomplished.

2. The *democratic* style is most desirable in that it allows the group to partake in the decision-making process. However, it still means that the leader is held accountable for the final decision.

3. In the *laissez-faire* style, the group is allowed to decide what they will do regarding a specific circumstance and the assigned leader simply follows along.

Patterns of Leadership

In addition to the styles of leadership, five patterns of leadership emerge.

1. *Telling* resembles the authoritarian method. This method works well in cases where an immediate decision must be made; however, there is not much need for this in social recreation.

2. *Selling* is when a leader attempts to convince the group that the particular task or event at hand will be beneficial or enjoyable to them.

3. In *testing*, the leader stands before the group and asks them if the would be willing to do what he or she suggests.

4. *Consulting* is when the leader first checks with select members of the group regarding a decision to be made, before actually presenting the decision to the group at large.

5. *Joining* is similar to laissez-faire, where the leader merely takes a member's role and does what the group as a whole has decided.

The Role of the Leader

The role of the leader is affected most by time constraints, the setting or environment, and the composition of the group members. Keeping an eye on the time is largely the responsibility of the leader; in addition, the timing of presenting activities and the timing between activities is crucial to success. This requires a certain amount of sensitivity. The setting or environment can make a major difference as to whether or not a program can meaningfully be carried out (e.g., if a leader was to try to get the attention of willing participants outdoors where it is very difficult to hear, or to handle paper and pencil, or maintain the attention of the attendees, it would be quite difficult to conduct a successful social recreation program). The author recommends that for a large proportion of social recreation programs the activities are much more successful outdoors. The composition of the group members has a major impact on the success of the leader. If the leader is not perceived as being fair to all participants, if he or she cannot maintain discipline and control of the group, if the group members have some particular needs for special attention and are disruptive, or if the group members show no self-control nor want to spend the time together in this particular group, then this will adversely affect the role of the leader. This is not to say that social recreation and its leader cannot overcome these problems. In fact, there are very few other disciplines that will permit those who are discontent with leaders or group members to amiably get along with one another.

Also very important in social recreation are the expectations of the participants. It is implicit that the reason for having social recreation program activities is to have fun. For some individuals, the interpretation of fun can be very different from that of the leader. Nonetheless, in the case of social recreation, once participants understand the goals and objectives—that the true fundamental purpose of social recreation is to get to meet others and form bonds with others and make friendships, to share in the leadership, develop personal worth, and have the opportunities for emotional release and relaxation, and to develop constructive group relationships and group morale and cohesion—they then look forward to future meetings with the same leader and group. The role of the leader should be that of a catalyst, an organizer, a mobilizer, a resource person, and a facilitator.

Instructions for Leading Activities or Games

"Dos"

1. Prepare the necessary materials (if any). Rehearse the introduction and the transition between the various phases of the game.
2. Motivate and condition the group with words of encouragement (e.g., explanations as to how much you have enjoyed the activity).
3. Take the starting formation (e.g., standing, sitting, circle, line or relay formation, partners, aggregate).
4. Explain and demonstrate the initial movements.
5. Ask select participants to practice (i.e., walk through) the activity.
6. Begin or play the game by using a signal or recognizable phrase (e.g., "ready, set, begin").
7. End the game or activity using a statement or signal. In games that do not have an obvious built-in ending, announce to the group that there will be one more time/turn/chance before the last round.

"Don'ts"

1. Never show signs of disparagement, or discourage individuals who do not wish to participate, and never feel disheartened if they do not engage in the activity. Not all persons will enjoy all activities at all times. However, keep in mind that your chief task as leader is to motivate and mobilize the group to interact.
2. Never lose eye contact with the group members.
3. Never talk down to the group or speak in a derogatory fashion. Always speak in a loud clear voice.

Specific Practical Leadership Techniques

While much of social recreation includes extensive leadership skills and techniques, the activities included in this book have been selected because they do not require special talents, abilities, or charisma. The following techniques are recommended as practical ways to organize and control a social recreation group:

- To organize a large number of people (i.e., twelve to thirty), particularly when they are outdoors, the most efficient way to is to ask that they join hands in a circle. From this position the leader can form smaller groups or other formation patterns.
- To divide a large seated audience into four small groups indoors, the most efficient way is to ask select individuals by name to form a circle in one of the four corners of the room. For example, the leader would say, "Everyone from Jim to Jane please form a circle in the corner over there." Be sure to include whether the group should be seated or standing.
- To quiet a large group of persons who are talking you can (a) say "May I have your attention please," (b) use a signal, such as raising your arm, or (c) flick the light switch.
- To gradually attract the attention of potential participants, begin with one or two members of the group using an entertaining activity that will eventually grab the entire group's attention (e.g., Stirrers Trick, Ring-String Trick, or Coins on a Napkin).

- Another way to begin a program of activities is to first distribute activity sheets, or passive games, to pairs of individuals seated in the group and ask that they work together to come up with the correct answers (e.g., Know the States, Numbers Association Challenge, University Entrance Exam).
- To organize groups/teams quickly and efficiently, request that individuals divide according to birthdays. For example, create the following three groups: January to April, May to August, and September to December.

In each of these examples, keep in mind the following points:

- Speak in a loud, clear voice.
- Maintain eye contact with the group members.
- Make announcements brief and to the point.
- Introduce the activities by stating their purpose, and include the reason that you believe they would enjoy doing these activities.
- In general, use names rather than numbers for setting up teams or small groups.
- Combine passive activities, primarily conducted while seating, and active activities (e.g., those done standing).

Functions of a Leader

Leaders function as organizers. They may often serve as role models for the group. Often they assist the group in setting goals and in making policies or rules. Social recreation leaders, in some situations, act as disciplinarians. They do not punish participants, but they attempt to guide them in the right direction. Often when individuals have difficulties with specific matters related to the activities, the leader will serve as a counselor. The leader frequently helps members, and the groups themselves, in evaluating their processes.

Evaluation

Evaluation is a process that most often utilizes some measurement device or tool to ascertain the effectiveness and quality of leadership and activities. Evaluation means making a determination regarding several issues that confront leaders. Most often, evaluation takes place for special events. Program activities and clubs do not receive the same scrutiny as does evaluation of special events. The evaluation of a recreation program can include adherence to rules and regulations, the ability of the leader to manage equipment, supplies, departmental forms, money, as well as public and community relations. Evaluation of a leader may be in terms of a review or rating. Evaluation usually means a judgment is to be made. Effectiveness and efficiency must be examined in the evaluation process. Items to consider for evaluation include the following:

1. Did the leader adequately plan and prepare for the event?

2. Was the leader enthusiastic and able to motivate others well?

3. Was the leader an effective organizer, giving clear directions in a loud, clear voice?

4. Was the leader able to maintain discipline and control?

5. Was the leader patient and persevering in overcoming problems?

Chapter Three
Group Dynamics

Group dynamics is the study of what happens in a group in terms of social interaction. It is an attempt to understand group behavior. It examines how people relate with one another, what kinds of friendships or cliques are formed, and what leadership techniques are used. Often, social climate and productivity of the group are examined. The principles of group dynamics have been widely used to develop effective group processes in various educational, governmental, and business organizations. Group dynamics has been used to improve leadership ability and to develop techniques for facilitation of group activities and effective group management.

The definition of a group is two or more individuals who interact with one another and share common goals, values, or interests. Group members must perceive themselves as being a group, and they must recognize a degree of interdependence exists among them—that they share common needs and aspirations. A setting where numerous people abound, but are not interacting with each other, is referred to as an aggregate.

There are different levels of groups, as there are different levels of cohesion. Typically, groups are said to be either formal or informal. The formal group is comprised of those individuals with whom one is employed, and the informal group is usually made up of those individuals who meet on a casual basis during leisure.

Some of the more common types of groups are families, social clubs, church congregations, union locals, political parties, college fraternities, armed forces units, gangs, and teams. Sociologists often refer to compulsory groups, such as families, religious groups, or prisoners. Persons in these groups are individuals who do not have much choice in the group to which they belong. For group members to be able to relate closely to one another there should be no more than ten to twelve members. While many groups do exist for an extended period of time, the length is not as important as the relationship. Group members are often able to accomplish together what they could not do individually, particularly in terms of problem solving.

Group development occurs in four stages: forming, storming, norming, and performing. *Forming* refers to the very beginning phase that occurs when members of a group meet for the first time. The objectives of the group are often unclear, the number of members a group desires to accept may be a question, and issues might arise regarding the homogeneous or heterogeneous nature of the group. *Storming* is the stage when much adjusting among group members occurs. It is a time when some individuals may decide they do not want to belong to that group, or if the group is poorly developed, the group itself may dissolve. *Norming* is when standards are being set, and objectives are well-formulated. *Performing* is the final stage when there is a leveling, and when in fact members understand their roles, and tasks get accomplished. It is a maintenance stage.

A tool for measuring group interaction, potential group productivity, and leadership is a sociogram. Sociometrics are devices used by group workers to understand what is happening in a group situation or activity. A good example of a sociogram is "First Impressions" (see Chapter Four), where participants demonstrate their willingness to participate in a group activity, and the number of responses on the cards placed on their backs reveals the level of their activity, as well as leadership potential. Another example would be when a group gathers together, is seated in a circle, or around a table, and begins to speak. There could be a given topic of discussion or not. An observer would draw a diagram on a sheet of paper with all the members, and then arrows connecting the speakers to one another. This would be conducted within a given time frame, such as five minutes. After the given time there then would be several arrows drawn to one particular individual in the group. This may be an indicator that this person could become the leader of the group. The diagram could also show that one or more individuals are withdrawing from the group or do not want to interact with this group. The sociogram is but a tool to indicate probable group effectiveness.

Group dynamics is centered primarily within the discipline of social psychology. However, it has been used in other areas of study, such as social work, rehabilitation services, and personnel management, and it certainly has practical implications for recreation workers.

In social recreation, group dynamics provides a basis for helping participants reach their fullest potentials by accepting themselves and others and playing effective roles within the group structure. This field of study first evolved during the 1930s when groups were used heavily in social work settings and rehabilitative situations, often within a psychoanalytical framework. In the late 1940s into the 1950s a rather new direction began, that is, the use of groups in staff development—the T-group or Sensitivity Training approaches.

A prominent name in the area of group dynamics is Kurt Lewin, who developed many of the ideas surrounding Sensitivity Training/T-Groups and Encounter Groups. Many of his studies took place at the Esalen Institute in California, a center of experimentation in human growth processes. During this developmental period of the 1950s into the 1960s, which typically became known as the Human Potential Movement, many organizations adopted the patterns of Kurt Lewin and utilized other extensions of similar ideas, namely, Assertiveness Training and Transactional Analysis.

Understanding Group Behavior

Basically, there are four ways to study human behavior: (a) collecting and analyzing existing products (frequently used by historians and biographers), (b) asking people questions (e.g., questionnaires and interviews), (c) watching people/observation, and (d) manipulating conditions (e.g., experimenting).

The determinants of group behavior include the following: the composition of the members, the setting/spatial arrangements, the nature of the task, the group climate/atmosphere, the philosophy of the leader, one's professional peers, the reward systems, the expectations of the participants, and, of course, time.

In the attempt to understand group behavior, some key characteristics of groups emerge. The first is to consider whether there are few members or many members; second is to consider whether the group is open (has a changing membership) or is closed (i.e., has a stable membership); and thirdly, the homogeneity or homogeneity of the group. The following chart should help in understanding the effects of these characteristics.

Group Characteristic	Effects
Few members	More cohesiveness and satisfaction, better communication
Many members	More creative ideas, more domination by individuals, more likely to have a leader
Open membership	More tolerant, shorter time together
Closed membership	Quicker to organize, longer time together
Heterogeneity of members	More flexibility, more creativity
Homogeneity of members	More satisfaction, more cohesiveness

Key Terms

Some key terms regarding group characteristics include the following:

- autonomy—how much a group functions independently of others
- cohesiveness—when a group holds together and when members identify with the purpose/values
- morale—the level of optimism about a group, and how members feel that it's meeting their needs
- norms—the standards or values of the group; approved ways of behaving
- permeability—the degree of difficulty involved in joining a group
- stratification—the extent to which group members are placed in clearly marked categories or subgroups that indicate their statuses

Recreation Facility Visit and Interview

Make arrangements to visit a professional recreation services facility that offers social recreation events (e.g., municipal recreation department, Boys/Girls Club, senior citizens center, YMHA/YWHA, YMCA/YWCA, 4-H Club, Boys Scouts or Girl Scouts, neighborhood association, armed forces service club, student activities office). You will not be able to use a therapeutic recreation site to complete this assignment. Do not use a hospital, nursing home, or treatment center. In most cases, you will not be able to use a commercial recreation site, such as a fitness center or health spa.

Use the outline on the following page to make observations and report on the recreation services made available by the agency you have visited. Do not include information on sports or sport equipment. Write out your answers in an essay format, copying each question with your responses. Be sure to include the name and complete address of the facility, the name of the recreation director, and the name, telephone number, and title of the person interviewed.

Recreation Staff
- How many full-time staff are employed for social recreation programming? part-time?
- What are their titles?
- What are their qualifications?

Recreation Program
- Where is the schedule or calendar of events located or posted?
- Does the program include activities at a variety of hours?
- What are the social recreation activities offered during the day? during the evenings? weekends? holidays?
- What are the most successful social recreation activities. Why?
- Which are the least popular activities? Why?
- Are the activities appropriate to the characteristics of the population? Why?
- Is there a good balance between the three levels of activities (i.e., program activities, clubs, and special events)?
- Describe the mixture of activities. Do the activities cover the range of activities categories (e.g., music, informal dramatics, dance, games)? Explain.
- What is the proportion of group to individual activities?

Clients
- How many clients are being served by this agency?
- What are the approximate demographics (in percentages) of the following: race/ethnicity? marital status? gender? disabled clients? age range?
- How many clients actually participate (i.e., active participants) in the social recreation program activities?
- How many members do not actually participate in the social recreation program activities? List the major reasons.

Physical Structure and Design
- How many rooms or areas are designed for purposes of social recreation (i.e., nonsport) activities?
- To what degree is barrier-free design utilized?
- What equipment and supplies are used for social recreation programming?
- How are bulletin boards used, if any?

General Comments and Evaluation
-
-
-

Chapter Four
Social and Group Games

The following activities are intended for at least six participants. In general, the most fun is generated when there are six to twelve participants. Please note the following arrangement is repeated throughout the book: title, category in italics, materials, formation, and directions.

Mixers and Icebreakers

Name Bingo

Competition

Note: This activity works best with a minimum of twelve participants

Materials: One piece of paper and pen/pencil for each participant

Formation: classroom seating or parlor style

Directions: Ask participants to draw lines on their papers to make a Bingo Card. The number of lines depends on the number of participants. Once this drawing is completed, participants are then asked to stand, exchange names, introduce themselves, and write the first and last name (or just first name) of the person they've met in any box. This continues until all of the boxes are filled with names. The names must be written by the player—do not collect autographs. Once the names have been collected on the grid, players take a seat. The leader begins by calling out one of the group

 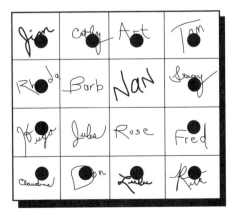

Examples of "Around the World" style of winning
(12-player card and 16-player card)

member's names. Players then cross out that name on their Bingo board. The player who has crossed out all of the outside boxes "around the world"—wins!

Friendship

Competition

Materials: at least ten envelopes with ten of the same letters in them—written on small index cards. One envelope has F, another R, another I, another E, and so forth—until the word friendship can be spelled.

Directions: Distribute the envelopes to the participants. Ask them to check to be sure there are ten of the same letters in their envelope. The object of this game is to spell the word "friendship." When the leader gives the signal, the participants are free to trade their letters with the others to spell out the word "friendship." Participants circulate among the group members to find who has the letters they need to spell the word "friendship." They meet, mingle, barter, and exchange letters. The first person to collect all ten letters is the winner.

First Impressions

Free Play

Materials: 5 x 8 index cards, scotch tape, pens/pencils

Formation: classroom seating

Directions: The leader and a helper tape a blank index card on the backs of all participants. He or she then asks everyone to stand and write their first impressions on those index cards on the backs of each participant. After a given time period, four minutes for a group of twenty-eight, everyone is asked to stop writing and take their seats. They then may remove the cards from their backs. Usually kind and flattering statements are made, although sometimes there are some humorous ones. Volunteers can read their cards to the group.

Names on Backs

Free Play

Materials: index cards with well-known celebrities or political figures written on them must be prepared in advance. Scotch tape is also needed.

Formation: Participants should be seated. Cards with well-known people's names are taped to their backs.

Directions: After everyone has had an index card taped to their back, the leader then asks all to stand and ask various members of the group to figure out who they are. Ask questions such as the following: Am I alive or dead? I am a female singer? Am I a male actor? Am I a historical figure? There is much activity among group members once each person begins asking questions. The leader must ensure that participants circulate to others to get "new ideas" and not get caught up in cliques.

Mixer of the Unknown

Free Play
Materials: index cards, pens/pencils
Directions: The leader distributes the cards and asks that everyone write something personal about himself or herself that no one in the room would know. He or she then collects the cards, mixes them, and redistributes them. He or she then asks everyone to stand and try to find the person who wrote the statement on the card they now hold. When the group stands there is a lot of interaction and much humor as an exchange of personal identities and information is passed.

Mind Bogglers (Mental Games)

Nine Times Table

Competition and Instruction
Formation: audience or classroom seating, or for a small group of six, seating at a round table. It is helpful to have a chalkboard if the group is made up of more than six people, otherwise this can be done with just a pen/pencil and paper.
Directions: The leader asks if there is someone in the group who feels confident working with numbers, math, or calculations. Once the individual with math skills is identified, the leader then announces that this activity will be a contest, a race, to see who can be faster at completing the nine times table. Ask the chosen individual to begin reciting the nine times table (9 x 1 = 9, 9 x 2 = 18, 9 x 3 = 27, and so on). At the same time he or she is reciting, the leader writes 0–9 vertically on the board (or paper) and then repeats the same in reverse (see box).

0	9
1	8
2	7
3	6
4	5
5	4
6	3
7	2
8	1
9	0

Without failure, the leader who writes the series of numbers will win the race. This will nicely surprise the group and is good way to then engage the group in the next activity.

11 Times 2 Digits (Up to 9)

Competition and Instruction
Materials: large piece of paper (8.5 x 11) or chalkboard, pens/pencils
Formation: sitting
Directions: As in the preceding activity ask for a volunteer or select someone in the group to multiply 23 by 11 as quickly as possible. Most individuals have difficulty doing this quickly. The leader illustrates the following: 23 x 11 and then points out that the quickest way to do this is to take the two numbers being multiplied by 11 and place the first of the two numbers on the left in the total; then place the second number, being multiplied by 11, on the right side of the total. In the center of those two numbers (in this case, 2 and 3), place the sum of those two numbers—which is 5.

Again, take the sum of 2 and 3 and place it in between the two numbers (2 and 3). This then will give you the solution. Demonstrate this again with another pair of numbers, such as 11 x 45, to offer a further example to the group. The answer is 495. Once again the two numbers being multiplied by 11 are added together and that sum is placed in the center of the two numbers (being multiplied by 11). Explain that this can be done only up to a combination of numbers whose total is no more than 9 digits.

Five- and Three-Gallon Containers

Materials: piece of paper (8.5 x 11) and pens/pencils, or chalkboard/chalk
Formation: sitting
Directions: Ask participants to figure out how to fill a five-gallon container with precisely four gallons, when all they have are a three-gallon container and five-gallon container and endlessly running water. You might say this is done at Niagara Falls, so that the concept of endlessly running water is made clear. Participants engage in a friendly interchange of ways to solve the problem.

Solution

1. Fill the five-gallon container.
2. Pour three gallons from the five-gallon container into the three-gallon container.
3. Pour out those three gallons.
4. Pour the two gallons of water that remained in the five-gallon container into the three-gallon container.
5. Fill up the five-gallon container to the top again.
6. Pour one gallon into the three-gallon container to fill it up to the top, making it three gallons.
7. This then leaves four gallons in the five-gallon container.

Three Men in a Hotel

Materials: piece of paper (8.5 x 11) and pens/pencils, or chalkboard/chalk
Formation: participants should be seated
Directions: The leader tells the story: Three men walk into a hotel and each spends $10.00 for one hotel room. The desk clerk sends them upstairs with the bellboy to the first room on the right. The hotel manager comes into the hotel and asks the clerk, "How's business?" The clerk answers, "Fine—I just rented the room upstairs on the right for $30.00." The manager then replies, "No, that's wrong, that room should only be $25.00, return $5.00 to them." He turns around and walks away. The clerk then calls the bellboy, and gives him five single dollars to return to the three men. On the way upstairs, the bellboy says to himself, "How do I divide $5.00 among three men?" He then gave them back each a $1.00 and kept $2.00 for himself. This means that the three men each paid $9.00 ($9.00 x 3 = $27.00) and the bellboy kept $2.00 for himself ($27.00 + $2.00 = $29.00). What happened to the extra dollar (that would make this equal the original $30.00)? Participants engage in a friendly interchange of methods to solve the problem.

Solution

Participants will be confused by the way the problem is posed. The solution is simply to present the situation another way. Participants should be reminded that multiplication or division cannot be combined with addition and subtraction. State that the room costs $25.00, and each man did receive $1.00 (that's $3.00 total), and the bellboy kept $2.00 for himself. All the figures are then added together to total $30.00 (25 + 3 + 2).

Aptitude Test

Materials: One copy of test per participant (top of page 44, making sure to cover the answers on the bottom), pens/pencils
Formation: sitting in classroom fashion
Directions: Participants simply write their responses on the sheets distributed. When completed, switch sheets to be "graded" by their classmates, or fellow participants. Participants respond aloud to each question demonstrating their "genius" and/or "ingenuity."

Know the States

Materials: One copy of test per group (page 45), pens/pencils
Formation: small groups of at least three sitting in a circle.
Directions: Ask each group to form a tight circle, sitting apart from the others, and out of hearing distance. Then fill in each of the states on the appropriate line. First team to finish all 50 states wins.

State Capitals

Competition
Materials: One copy of test (pages 46 and 47), pens/pencils
Formation: classroom seating or parlor seating
Directions: This activity works well as a supplement or follow up to Know the States. Once a pair or group completes the Know the States game, the leader would then have the winning team continue their "superior knowledge" by completing this more challenging activity. Participants fill in the states next to the given captitals.

University Entrance Exam (common American sayings/terms)

Materials: One copy of test (with answers covered) per group (page 48, and an enlarged photocopy is suggested for increased readability), pens/pencils
Formation: sitting in a small group circle (a minimum of three people) and out of hearing distance of other groups

Directions: Explain to the groups/teams that they are to decipher or decode the messages numbered on the sheet (cover up answers or suggest no peeking). The first team winning reads the answers aloud. Each group/team engages in a friendly interaction of eagerly trying to decipher the coded messages.

Apples and Oranges

Materials: a large piece of paper and pens/pencils for more than six participants, a chalkboard or writing board
Formation: seated
Directions: Draw three barrels or baskets. On one barrel write the letter A for apples, write an O for oranges on the other barrel, and write an A + O on the third barrel. Explain to the group that the barrels are *not* labeled correctly. Then ask them to place their hand inside one barrel, come up with one fruit, and tell everyone what is contained in each barrel. Much puzzlement and confusion usually takes place, causing many questions to be asked and many repeated answers. Eventually, players discover the logical, deductive reasoning involved.
Solution
The solution is to place your hand in the barrel marked A + O, take out one fruit, let's say it is an apple. If that barrel contains apples, and we know that the barrels are not marked correctly, then the barrel marked A for apples must contain the oranges; and therefore the barrel marked O must be the combination of A + O or apples and oranges.

Games Played While Seated in Groups of No More Than Five

Numbers Association Challenge

Materials: one copy of challenge per group (page 49), pens/pencils
Formation: seated; two or three individuals sitting near each other
Directions: Follow instructions on the printed sheet. Each person shares his or her reaction to the numbered items.

Categories

Materials: one piece of paper (8.5 x 11), pens/pencils for each group

Formation: minimum three groups (of three to five persons each) seated in each corner of the room
Directions: Organize the group into at least three teams and ask for one individual in each team to be an "honest scribe"—one who will not change the answers. Distribute the piece of paper to the teams' scribes, and inform the group that there must be only one answer in each box. Depending on how much time you would like this game to last, ask the group for someone whose name is three, four, or five letters long; the teams' scribes will then write those letters in each of the column boxes under the "Letter of the Alphabet." The rules of the game are each team must select a name that one of the other teams does not select, in order to earn the ten points each box is worth. Once all teams have completed the form, or that "time" has been called, the leader then asks the scribe in the first team to read his or her answer aloud for the first item (Girl's Name). Next, the scribe in the second team reads his or her team's answer aloud for Girl's Name, and then the next team's scribe reads his or her team's response for "Girl's Name." At this point, the leader asks all scribes to add up their scores and write them in the designated column. At the end of the game, each team is to tally their scores, the team with the most points wins.

Down Jacks

Materials: a long table and one quarter
Formation: two teams seated shoulder to shoulder, on each side of the table
Directions: One team is given the quarter to pass back and forth underneath the table to their team members. The opposite team looks into the opposing team's eyes while everyone on the quarter's team pretends they're passing the coin—whether or not they have it. When the leader calls out "Up Jacks" everyone in the team with the quarter raises their fists above the table, and Down Jacks is called by leader, everyone slams their hands down on the table to cover up the sound of the quarter hitting the table. The opposing team must guess who has the quarter. Repeat the same for the other team.

Bowling With Candles

Materials: a wooden board with holes drilled in the shape of a bowling pin triangle; ten candles to fit in the holes; a book of matches.

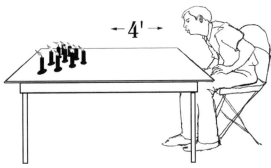

Formation: sitting in at least two teams
Directions: Leader or designee lights the ten candles. He then asks one team member at a time to sit before the lit candles on a table and take two tries to blow them out. Use the bowling scoring technique for scoring. Candles should be approximately four feet from the chair. Participants compete one at a time to have their team win.

Find It in the News

Materials: two identical newspapers, two pairs of scissors, two chairs, a table, and list of the newspaper headlines selected
Formation: two equal numbered teams seated at opposite ends of a table; a score keeper/judge reader is needed.
Directions: Two team members, one from each team begins by taking the contestants' seats and when the leader reads the Activity Title of the newspaper article, each contestant must search, find and neatly cut out the article and submit it to the judge. The first person to submit the article wins. Teams root for their team members (and should be encouraged to do so) while urging them to finish first in the race.

Five Ways to Conduct the Same Activity

A number of activities in this book (e.g., *Ad Phrases,* page 42; *Name the Nation,* page 72; and *Name That Tune,* page 73) lend themselves well to any one of the following methods of procedure.

1) **The Written-Passive Method**: Have participants write numbers on a sheet of paper (e.g., 1 through 5), then present the first part of the quiz. Once those five answers are written down, ask the group who completed the entire list, or who believes they have the most correct answers, and have that participant read his or her answers aloud. Proceed to the next group (e.g., 6 through 10), repeating the process.

2) **Raise Your Hand and Call Out the Answer**: As the questions are slowly read to the entire group, participants who wish to answer simply raise their hand, and once selected to answer, will call out the answer.

3) **At Least Two Teams**: Divide the participants into at least two groups/teams, keeping scores separated for each. This is similar to #2, where hands are raised and teams are chosen to give their answer(s).

4) **Team Contestants**: Set up chairs (one for each team) in front of the participants, and ask a contestant from each team to occupy one. Other team members are permitted to silently mouth the answers in an attempt to get him or her to respond correctly, and each contestant gets three guesses, at which time another team member may take the chair and continue guessing.

5) **First Team to Walk Up**: A set of keys, borrowed from one of the participants, is placed on a chair at the front of the groups. The questions are presented one at a time and for each one, the first person to walk up to the chair, place the keys in his or her hand and correctly answer, will score a point.

Other Competitive Group Games

Horse Racing

Competition
Materials: six cards, Ace, 2, 3, 4, 5, and 6; can also be played with dice (2) or with just using the other cards from the deck
Formation: Participants gathered around a table (preferably seated). The six playing cards are laid on the table as well as a "racetrack" made up of other playing cards, approximately nine cards separated, in line with one another.

Directions: Each person is asked which "horse" they would like to cheer for. If there are only six participants, then one person would get another ace from the deck, another person would get another 2 from the deck, a third person would get another 3 from the deck, and so on, until each player has a matching card for their horse. If dice are available, each player should have a chance to roll them. If the first person rolls a 2 and a 4, then the 2 and 4 horse start out first, each advancing one space. The second person rolls and tries to roll at least one of the dice in favor of moving his or her horse. If there are no dice available, simply place the six cards, Ace, 2, 3, 4, 5, 6, in a hat or bag mix and pick. This uses the same procedure, except that only one horse can move per card drawing. The participants usually get quite worked up rooting for their horse, hoping it will win. The leader may also set up a win, place, and show finale.

Gift Box and Music

Competition

Materials: At least five boxes of various sizes that fit into one another, some type of recorded music that is upbeat and fast

Formation: Participants should be seated in a circle. This activity is much more successful if there are no more than twelve players.

Directions: The leader must prepare the boxes in advance. Begin with the smallest box and place some wrapped candies, enough for each participant, in it. So if there are twelve players there should be at least twelve candies. Wrap that box up in wrapping paper or colorful newspaper. After wrapping,

place that box into the next box, and wrap that box (in either wrapping paper or newspaper funnies). Continue this for the remaining boxes, placing one inside the other and wrapping them. No one should know that there are several boxes wrapped inside one another, except you. The game then operates much like musical chairs. When the music begins playing, the participants seated in the circle begin to pass the large box. The rules are "when the music stops playing, the person holding the box must unravel and open it." Once the leader stops the music, the person left holding the box begins to unravel it, but, the leader then should continue the music before the box is completely unraveled. This allows for more participation and more activity. The timing is very important. Do not allow one person to completely open the box. Start and stop the music frequently. Of course, once the first box is opened and they find another, the game becomes more intriguing.

Ad Phrases

Competition

Materials: list of slogans, prepared in advance (page 43); paper and pens/pencils

Formation: This should be done with a larger group of approximately twelve to twenty-five participants.

Directions: This activity is fairly straightforward. The leader keeps score, reads the "questions" to the group and the group members respond. Refer to "Five Ways to Conduct the Same Activity" (page 40) for suggestions on procedure.

Questions/Answers

1. You're in good hands... (Allstate)
2. Soup is good food. (Campbell's)
3. They really satisfy. (Snickers)
4. Get a piece of the rock. (Prudential)
5. We build excitement. (Pontiac)
6. The quicker picker upper. (Bounty)
7. Don't leave home without it. (American Express)
8. Born and brewed in the USA. (Miller)
9. Reach out and touch someone. (AT&T)
10. Give me a light. (Bud Light)
11. When it absolutely, positively has to be there overnight. (Federal Express)
12. We do chicken right. (Kentucky Fried Chicken)
13. All the news that's fit to print. (New York Times)
14. Where more Americans find a bigger refund. (H&R Block)
15. Plop, plop, fizz, fizz... (Alka-Seltzer)
16. Snap, crackle, pop. (Rice Krispies)
17. Soup that eats like a meal. (Chunky)
18. No more ring around the collar. (Wisk)
19. Sometimes you feel like a nut, sometimes you don't. (Mounds/Almond Joy)
20. Where's the beef? (Wendy's)
21. Melts in your mouth, not in your hand. (M&M's)
22. A sprinkle a day helps keep odor away. (Shower to Shower)
23. Who could ask for anything more. (Toyota)
24. Good to the last drop. (Maxwell House)
25. They're unsinkable. (Cheerios)
26. Breakfast of champions. (Wheaties)
27. When it rains, it pours. (Morton)
28. We try harder. (Avis)
29. Does she...or doesn't she? (Clairol)
30. Look Ma, no cavities! (Crest)
31. Let your fingers do the walking. (Yellow Pages)
32. We bring good things to life. (General Electric)
33. Stronger than dirt. (Ajax)
34. A little dab'll do ya. (Brylcreem)
35. Please don't squeeze the... (Charmin)
36. The pause that refreshes. (Coca-Cola)

Aptitude Test (handout)

1. Do they have a fourth of July in England?
2. Some months have 30 days, some will have 31; how many months have 28?
3. I have in my hand two U.S. coins that total 55 cents in value. One is not a nickel. What are the two coins?
4. A farmer had 17 sheep. All but nine died. How many did he have left?
5. Divide 30 by 1/2 and add 10. What is the answer?
6. Two men play checkers. They play five games and each man wins the same number of games. There were no ties. How can this be?
7. Take two apples from three apples and what do you have?
8. An archaeologist claimed he found some gold coins dated 46 B.C. Do you think he did? Why?
9. How many animals of each species did Moses take into the Ark with him?
10. Is it legal in North Carolina for a man to marry his widow's sister?

Answers to Aptitude Test

1. Yes, a fourth…and a fifth…and a sixth…
2. All of them have 28 days
3. The answer is a fifty cents piece and a nickel (only one is not a nickel)
4. Nine
5. Remember the teachings of elementary school, we must invert the fraction when doing multiplication. So, it should be solved using 30 x 2/1 = 60, + 10 = 70
6. They were not playing the same players, they were playing different players.
7. You have two apples
8. No, no one could have known that Christ was to come 46 years later.
9. It wasn't Moses, it was Noah.
10. No, because he's dead.

Know the States (handout)

1. A _____	26. M _____
2. A _____	27. N _____
3. A _____	28. N _____
4. A _____	29. N _____
5. C _____	30. N _____
6. C _____	31. N _____
7. C _____	32. N _____
8. D _____	33. N _____
9. F _____	34. N _____
10. G _____	35. O _____
11. H _____	36. O _____
12. I _____	37. O _____
13. I _____	38. P _____
14. I _____	39. R _____
15. I _____	40. S _____
16. K _____	41. S _____
17. K _____	42. T _____
18. L _____	43. T _____
19. M _____	44. U _____
20. M _____	45. V _____
21. M _____	46. V _____
22. M _____	47. W _____
23. M _____	48. W _____
24. M _____	49. W _____
25. M _____	50. W _____

State Capitals (handout)

1. Montgomery   _____

2. Juneau   _____

3. Phoenix   _____

4. Little Rock   _____

5. Sacramento   _____

6. Denver   _____

7. Hartford   _____

8. Dover   _____

9. Tallahassee   _____

10. Atlanta   _____

11. Honolulu   _____

12. Boise   _____

13. Springfield   _____

14. Indianapolis   _____

15. Des Moines   _____

16. Topeka   _____

17. Frankfort   _____

18. Baton Rouge   _____

19. Augusta   _____

20. Annapolis   _____

21. Boston   _____

22. Lansing   _____

23. St. Paul   _____

24. Jackson   _____

25. Jefferson City   _____

State Capitals (handout)

26. Helena   _____

27. Lincoln   _____

28. Carson City   _____

29. Concord   _____

30. Trenton   _____

31. Santa Fe   _____

32. Albany   _____

33. Raleigh   _____

34. Bismarck   _____

35. Columbus   _____

36. Oklahoma City _____

37. Salem   _____

38. Harrisburg   _____

39. Providence   _____

40. Columbia   _____

41. Pierre   _____

42. Nashville   _____

43. Austin   _____

44. Salt Lake City _____

45. Montpelier   _____

46. Richmond   _____

47. Olympia   _____

48. Charleston   _____

49. Madison   _____

50. Cheyenne   _____

University Entrance Exam (handout)

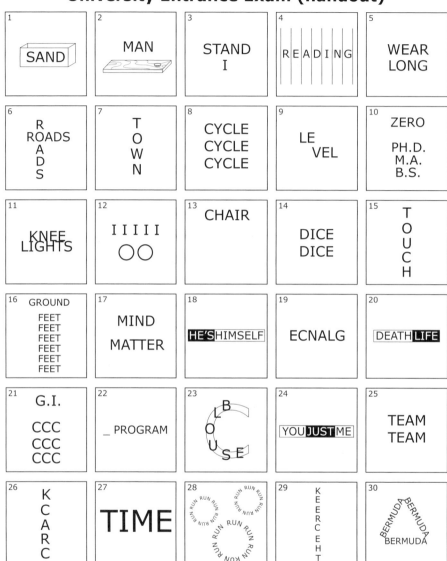

Answers:

1. sandbox
2. man overboard
3. I understand
4. reading between the lines
5. long underwear
6. crossroads
7. downtown
8. tricycle
9. bi-level or split level
10. three degrees below zero
11. neon lights
12. circles under the eyes
13. highchair
14. paradise (pair of dice)
15. touchdown
16. six feet under ground
17. mind over matter
18. he's beside himself
19. backward glance
20. life after death
21. G.I. overseas
22. space program
23. see-through blouse
24. just between you and me
25. double team
26. crack up
27. big time
28. run around in circles
29. up the creek
30. Bermuda triangle

Numbers Association Challenge (handout)

Instructions: Each question below contains the initials of words that will make it correct. Find the missing words.

Examples: 16 = O. in a P.   Ounces in a Pound
              26 = L. of the A.   Letters of the Alphabet

 1. 7 = W. of the A. W.
 2. 1,001 = A. N.
 3. 12 = S. of the Z.
 4. 54 = C. in a D. (with the J.)
 5. 9 = P. in the S. S.
 6. 88 = P. K.
 7. 13 = S. on the A. F.
 8. 32 = D. F. at which W. F.
 9. 18 = H. on a G. C.
10. 90 = D. in a R. A.
11. 200 = D. for P. G. in M.
12. 8 = S. on a S. S.
13. 3 = B. M. (S. H. T. R.)
14. 4 = Q. in a G.
15. 24 = H. in a D.
16. 1 = W. on a U.
17. 5 = D. in a Z. C.
18. 57 = H. V.
19. 11 = P. on a F. T.
20. 1,000 = W. that a P. is W.
21. 29 = D. in F. in a L. Y.
22. 64 = S. on a C.
23. 40 = D. and N. of the G. F.

Answers to Numbers Association Challenge

1. 7 wonders of the ancient world
2. 1,001 Arabian nights
3. 12 signs of the zodiac
4. 54 cards in a deck (with the jokers)
5. 9 planets in the solar system
6. 88 piano keys
7. 13 stripes on the American flag
8. 32 degrees Fahrenheit at which water freezes
9. 18 holes on a golf course
10. 90 degrees in a right angle
11. 200 dollars for passing go in Monopoly
12. 8 sides on a stop sign
13. 3 blind mice (see how they run)
14. 4 quarts in a gallon
15. 24 hours in a day
16. 1 wheel on a unicycle
17. 5 digits in a zip code
18. 57 Heinz varieties
19. 11 players on a football team
20. 1,000 words that a picture is worth
21. 29 days in February in a leap year
22. 64 squares on a checkerboard
23. 40 days and nights of the great flood

Chapter Five
Active Games

The following activities require the entire group to be standing. Many times, adult group members will be reticent and rather uncertain they want to stand for a group activity, particularly if they do not have a clear understanding as to what will happen once they do rise, or they are insecure because they do not know what to expect and fear something the leader will ask of them will cause them to exert themselves or be embarrassed. The fact of the matter is, a good social recreation leader will make it quite apparent to participants that they will not be singled out nor will they be asked to perform a specific skill as might be found in sports. Instead, participants soon learn that the activities described herein are simply casual experiences that have a certain familiarity and affectionate appeal built into them.

Human Sculpture

Competition

Formation: There should be a minimum of four groups, one in each corner of the room. The number of persons per group varies according to the size of the aggregate. If there are twelve persons, then each group would be made up of three persons. **Directions**: Each group is given approximately three minutes to decide among themselves what sculpture they can create, or act out. Naturally, it is a still life. When called on by the leader, each group will take their pose. The leader then will ask the other participants to guess what the sculpture is. If there are an uneven number of participants, then they may become judges to decide on the best sculpture.

Feather on a Sheet

Competition

Materials: a bedsheet (at least queen size) and a feather
Formation: one team stands on one side of the sheet and the other team on the opposite side, with referees on each end
Directions: The leader tosses the feather into the center of the sheet, and each team begins blowing to get the feather over the other team's side. Each team must stand fast and not move. Emphasize the rule that every participant must remain in his or

her place and not walk toward the center of the sheet. The entire group begins blowing hard and wild and some people lose their breath trying to restrain their laughter.

Sheet Soccer

Competition

Materials: a double or queen size sheet, with a hole cut out on each end; a ball

Directions: Two teams stand on opposite sides holding the very edge of the sheet, spread out. The leader drops the ball in the center of the sheet. Each team is to try to get the ball in the opposite hole. Everyone must continue to hold the very edge of the sheet and keep the sheet below his or her waistline. This game can become quite exciting and wild. Assertive leadership is needed to ensure rules are being followed.

Spoon Relay

Competition

Materials: three spoons and three rolls of string (with a length of at least seventy-five feet each)

Formation: standing in line, front to back in relay formation

Directions: Have teams line up in relay formation, front to back. Designate the first person of each team as Team Leader and give him or her a roll of string tied to a spoon. At the command, each person in the line must put the spoon (and string) down the neck of their clothing, take it out at the bottom of their skirt or pants and then pass it to the next person by pulling the string back, completely rolled-up by the leader. Participants compete in attempting to be the fastest team to go up and down, back and forth, through the entire team.

Overtake

Competition

Materials: any two similar objects of a different color (e.g., two balls, two balloons, or two empty plastic bottles)

Formation: standing in a circle

Directions: Announce two teams will be formed. Ask that they count off from one to the highest number in the group. Then ask all the persons with odd numbers to raise their hands. Give one color object to an odd-numbered team member and the other color object to an even-numbered team member. The even-numbered member should be facing the odd-numbered team member directly opposite him or her. Demonstrate the activity, explaining that one team's object is passed to their teammates only. The object is to overtake or pass over the other team's object. Opposing teams cannot prevent the object from being passed. The two teams hurriedly pass their object from one member to the next. As the object gets closer, the excitement heightens.

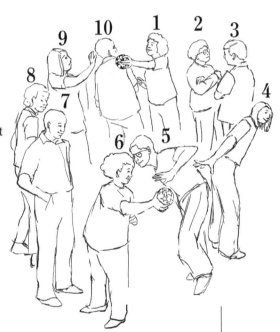

Steal the Object

Competition

Materials: an object to steal (e.g., a bottle cap, an empty soda can, a scarf, or handkerchief)

Formation: Two groups standing, in line, facing the other opposing team, approximately fifteen feet apart. Each group member on group/team A says a number beginning with one; next person, two; next person, three, until all team members have a number. The same pattern of counting numbers is done for the other team, but in the opposite direction. This way number one on team A is diagonally across from number one on team B. An object is placed in the center of the two teams.

Directions: The leader will announce a number. When that number is called the two opposing team members with that number walk out an attempt to take the object and bring it back to their team lineup without being tagged. After approximately four numbers are called, the leader can then call two numbers, at which time four individuals will walk out from their line up, and attempt to take the object back to their team's lineup. The team members that come to the center to take the object must be cautious not to be tagged. They might actually wait for the opposing team member to take the object so that they can tag them—and then receive the point. Also, team members might fake their intent to grab the object to spur the opposing team to grab the object first, only to be tagged "out." This game must be under careful watch so that no one gets hurt since some individuals try to be so fast that they lose control. It must be emphasized that participants are to walk out of their lineup and not run. This is one activity in which the leader must say, "This will be the last round, or last time," since there is no natural ending to the game.

Pocket and Purse Scavenger Hunt

Competition
Materials: list of items participants may have in their pockets or purses (e.g., a 1998 dime, a pocket telephone book, a driver's license)
Formation: audience seating, or table seating at a restaurant or picnic ground
Directions: At the start of the activity, the leader should divide the aggregate into four groups, being certain that there are approximately the same number of men and women in each. Dividing into four groups can be done efficiently because there are four corners to nearly every room. The leader establishes a post, such as a chair, in the center of the room, and asks for a volunteer to be a judge and scorekeeper at that post. The leader explains that he or she will announce certain items and the first group to bring that item to the post will receive a point for his or her group. It must be emphasized that there should be no running to the post—for safety. The leader then begins by calling out the items from the previously prepared list (which should include an odd number of items to prevent ties). The judge or scorekeeper verifies that the item brought to him or her is correct and notes which group receives the point.

Balloon Basketball

Competition

Materials: balloons, chairs, card deck (optional)

Formation: Teams A and B (with at least six participants per team) are seated approximately three feet apart, facing one another so that there is a open aisle between them. If it is cumbersome and you need assistance to create two teams, pairing can be accomplished by using a deck of cards. Give all participants a card from the deck ensuring that each one gets a black or a red card that will equally divide the group. Then ask that those with a black card sit side-by-side on the right, and those with a red card sit on the left.

Directions: The leader selects the person seated in the last seat of Team A to be the "basket" for his or her team. Likewise, the person seated at the end of Team B is asked to stand and be the basket for Team B. The basket holds his or her arms out in the shape of a basket. Both teams are asked to use only their left hands; all right hands should be placed behind their backs. The rules are that there is no blocking, no standing, and of course, use of only one hand. The leader, who has one balloon that he or she will tap up in the air in the center of the two teams, says that the team that can score in their team's basket, gets the point. The leader should have a spare balloon or two in case the balloon pops. Both groups are encouraged to engage in teamwork to get the balloon to gently "float" down their side of the aisle to their team's basket. The human basket often bends and stretches to accommodate the intended point.

Balloon Soccer

Competition

Materials: balloons, chairs

Formation: Two lines of chairs (no more than twelve on each line) are set up facing one another approximately three feet apart, so as to form an aisle down the middle. The participants are asked to sit on the chairs next to one another. One line becomes one team, and the other line another team. It is advisable to ask each line to give themselves a team name. This helps boost enthusiasm and team morale. One member from each team (the last seated in the line) is asked to be a scorer and a retriever, and stand behind their team.

Directions: The leader announces that the team who can tap the balloons over the heads of their opponents will score one point. The scorer/retriever keeps score for their team. The leader then takes one (or more) balloons and taps it (or them—depending on the number of participants) in the center of the two teams. The leader must emphasize that teamwork is the best way to score points, as the participants attempt to swat the balloon(s) over the heads of the opposing team. This activity can be done with just one balloon, but is more fun with more than one. The scorers retrieve the balloons when they fall to the floor and tap them into the center of the two teams.

Volleyball Balloons

Competition

Materials: balloons, chairs, string (approximately five to six feet in length)

Formation: This activity has a different formation than the preceding two activities. The two teams must be sitting in chairs, in rows, one behind the other, facing the opposing team. One member from each team is asked to come and hold a string—to be the "net."

Directions: The two persons holding the "net" are told they may raise and lower the string to assist their team. The game is played very much like a real volleyball game, though play- ers are seated. There is much competitive fervor that occurs in this game as participants attempt to hit the balloon much as they would an actual volleyball.

Balloons in the Air

Competition

Materials: balloons

Formation: Participants stand together, arms stretched out, hand-to-shoulder, to form a circle. In addition, there must be a monitor/observer who will assist in administering the balloon at the appropriate time.

Directions: The leader informs the groups that when the monitor holds the balloon up high in the center of their circle they are to keep the balloon up in the air by blowing. They must coordinate their efforts to keep the balloon up in the air the longest to be the winning team. This can be quite a diffi- cult task as the participants generally find themselves laughing hysterically.

Chapter Six
Demonstration or Entertainment
Activities

One extremely popular category of social recreation is demonstration or entertainment. Here the leader of the group, takes on the role of "performer" or entertainer, and allows the group, or audience, to play a less active role in the actual presentation of fun activities. Because it is social recreation though, the leader should always try to involve the group or audience as much as possible. This is done by asking for volunteers and utilizing as many group members as possible.

Rope Trick

Entertainment

Materials: clothesline rope (approximately 18 to 24 inches in length)
Formation: seated at tables, classroom seats, or in a living room
Directions: The leader takes out a rope, or ropes, and asks the group for a "volunteer" to tie a square knot in the center without letting go of the two ends! It must be made clear that the ends must not be held with fingertips, so that all can see there is no mischievous manipulation. Several participants should come before the group, and demonstrate their idea as to how this should be done. The solution is to cross your arms first, pick up the two ends, and pull—straightening out the arms, to tie the knot.

Ring String Trick

Entertainment

Materials: string (approximately 36 inches in length)
Formation: group seated at tables or in a living room
Directions: The leader asks the group for an assistant to hold up her fists and extend her thumbs. He also asks that she or another woman allow them to use a small, smooth, finger ring for this trick. On her thumbs he places a string tied together with one knot. He then takes one side off to place the ring on the center of the string. Then he challenges the individuals of the group to come before the group and "take the ring off the string without taking the string off the thumbs."

This activity is the most difficult of all those printed in this book, and thus, requires practice on behalf of the presenter. A series of humorous actions occur when members of the group are encouraged by the leader to offer their ideas as to how this trick can be done. The solution is to first hold your hands as though you were to clap them, then place them back-to-back with the right hand on top. Insert this position into the center of the string, on the right-hand side of the ring. Pull up with the right, and down with the left, then criss-cross them. With the left hand now on top, place left side of the string over the left thumb of the assistant so that it is held there. Do not let go of the string in the right hand. Then take the string on your left side of the ring and wrap that around the assistant's left thumb again. Instruct the assistant to "say the magic words" as you then tug lightly on the ring while the assistant is left standing with the tied string on her thumbs!

Couple String Trick

Entertainment

Materials: two pieces of string (each approximately 18 inches in length)

Formation: Two members of the audience (one male and one female) are asked to participate. They then come up, standing before the entire group. The leader takes the two strings and ties the female member's wrists with each end of one string. The leader then takes one of the male member's wrists and ties it with the other string. The leader now takes the end of that same string and slips it under and over the female member's string (between her wrists) to use the string—attached to the male's wrist, to tie up the male member's wrist. The results are that the couple appear to be handcuffed together.

Directions: Once the two members are tied up the leader stands back and asks the group to help these two individuals wiggle out of this predicament. This activity follows the Ring String Trick very well. So, the leader should remind everyone of the way the ring was removed from the string in the previous activity. There is much hilarity that ensues once the audience members attempt to give directions to the couple as to how to get out of the situation. The leader should continually encourage group participation in the name of new ideas. There then should be a lot of twisting and turning on behalf of the couple, and the leader should only encourage more activity.

After approximately ten minutes, the leader can ask the group if they would like to see the solution. The solution is much simpler than the Ring-String Trick. Simply take the higher hand/wrist, the one where the string on one participant is above the other participant's hand, slip the center of the string over the lower wrist's string and then tuck it under the string, pull it through enough to then wrap it around that same hand. Ask the participant to say the magic words and voilà! they are free from one another.

Nine Nails Balanced on One

Free Play or Entertainment
Materials: nine nails and one other hammered into a piece of wood. The best size are tenpenny nails.
Formation: Audience or classroom seating, or, this activity will work well at a picnic or barbecue. The leader places a nail hammered into a piece of wood onto a table for all to see. There really should be no more than twelve partici- pants for this, although it is possible to do it successfully with up to twenty- five.

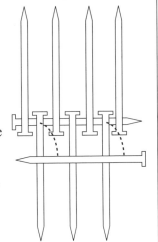

Directions: The leader challenges the group to figure out how to balance nine nails on the head of the one nail ham- mered into the wood. The leader usu- ally must ask for several contestants to give it a try. After several participants come up to the table to try, the leader can then offer the actual solution.

Solution

First you must lay one nail flat on the table. Secondly, take another nail and lay it perpendicularly across the other, with the head of the nail lying close to the stem of the first nail (that is laying flat on the table). Take a third nail and lay it perpendicular to the first nail, in the same way as the sec- ond nail, but, in the opposite direction. Continue this pattern until seven nails are lying (perpendicularly) on the first nail. Take the ninth (last) nail and lay it on top of the eight nails, between their heads, parallel to the first nail. This last nail must lay in the opposite direction so that the head of the first nail and the head of the ninth nail are on opposite sides. Now pinch the two ends of the first and ninth nail, pick them up and place them center on the head of the hammered nail.

How to Levitate

Entertainment
Formation: audience or restaurant-style seating
Directions: The leader asks for four strong young ladies to volunteer and one male who weighs approximately 165 pounds. The leader provides an armless chair for the male to sit—facing the audience. The four ladies are asked to clasp their two hands together with the thumb and index fingers pointing, or extended. Two ladies are then asked to hold this position under the knees of the male. The other two ladies are asked to hold the extended finger position under the shoulders of the male. The male is asked if he has ever been levitated before. Most likely he has not.

At this time, the leader must ask the audience for their complete cooperation by keeping totally silent. The male is asked to relax. The ladies are told that at the count of three, they will attempt to lift the man up. In all probability, he will not be lifted. Now, the leader instructs the young ladies to drop their hands. The leader asks one lady to hold her right hand palm down, above the head of the seated male being sure not to touch the head. The next lady is asked to place her hand in the same fashion above the first lady's hand—without touching. The third and fourth ladies are asked to do the same—without touching. This same approach is to be taken with the left hand for each lady. The man is asked to concentrate, and close his eyes because now he will be levitated.

The four ladies are now asked to get back in their original positions, holding their hands in the same fashion. The leader reminds the audience that there must be total silence and that the male should concentrate. The leader then says to the ladies, "okay on the count of three, we will levitate him." The leader counts to three, and lo and behold the man is levitated! Most often, the audience members, or even the young ladies, wonder why the man was lifted the second time and not the first. The leader can say that it is just a matter of dynamic tension.

Stirrers Trick

Demonstration or Entertainment
Materials: five plastic stirrers and a book of matches
Formation: seated at a dining room table
Directions: The leader asks a participant to light a match. He
or she then takes two of the five stirrers and crosses them
about two-thirds from the bottom to make an X. He or she
holds the plastic stirrer over the flame and then melts them
together. After a quick moment the plastic is cool enough to
press the two together to ensure a secure bond. The leader
then takes another stirrer and lays it on top of the X. This
will allow the three stirrers to stand alone. The leader now
challenges any member from the group to take the remaining stirrer and lift all three with just the one stirrer—without
changing its shape. The rules are that the straight stirrer cannot be bent, heated or cut. In one story, it was said that this
configuration was used by nomadic Indian tribes who had
to quickly depart on their migration adventures. The leader
must sometimes turn the remaining stirrer over to a potential
contestant and ask him, or her, to "Give it a try," repeating the
phrase, "The object is to lift the three stirrers with just the one
(remaining) stirrer—nothing more." This activity makes for
much intrigue and mystery as to how this can be done. The
solution is to take the three stirrers and arrange them so that
the two welded together are closest to you, and the loose stirrer is pointed toward you. Place the remaining, loose stirrer in
the center of the single unwelded stirrer; then while blowing
gently at the top of the configuration, pull gently inward with
the loose-single stirrer. This then allows the loose stirrer to
flip over, catching itself in the crux of the two welded stirrers.
Thus the shape of the original configuration is maintained and
all participants are in awe that this could be done!

Coins on a Napkin

Demonstration or Entertainment
Materials: This activity requires an accomplice. It is done on
a dining room table with two napkins, a drinking glass, and
five quarters.
Directions: The leader announces to the group that he or she
has developed a very sensitive touch and that it can be demonstrated by placing five quarters on a napkin. It is advisable

to get the quarters from the participants themselves. Once the napkins are arranged so that there is one in the center and the other four are in each corner of the napkin, the leader says he would like someone to hold his or her finger down on one of the quarters and count to ten aloud, while the leader turns his or her head (or walks away). When the leader turns around (or returns) she or he takes two fingers and hovers over the quarters—without touching any. The leader will know which quarter it is when the shill takes a drink from his or her glass and places it on the same exact corner where the quarter was touched, or if the center quarter was selected then the glass would go in the center of his or her napkin. The group is in awe with this activity because they cannot understand how one could have such incredible powers as to hover over a quarter and tell which was chosen. They often believe it is the heat (caused by pressing down on the coin for five seconds) that creates rays of energy. This activity can be done several times without detection—particularly if the accomplice is coy and cunning.

Tavern Puzzle

Demonstration or Entertainment

Materials: There are several varieties of this sort of puzzle. An outstanding one is a pair of horseshoes that are welded together by a ring. These are available commercially these days in many game or hobby stores, museum shops, tourist shops, and festivals.

Formation: This could be done in a small group or audience seating

Directions: The leader challenges any member of the group to take the ring off the two connecting horseshoes. After one or two participants try, the leader can then show how it is done. Several participants are asked to try, after the leader demonstrates the skill. The solution is to twist the horseshoes in opposite directions while shaking the ring so that it will fall in the center. Once it falls in between one horseshoe, the ring will slip over that horseshoe and the leader can now take it off, hold it up so that all the group can see. It spurs other participants to really want to try so they can figure it out and do it.

Chapter Seven
Noncompetitive Group Games

These activities, also known as "new games," have a couple of advantages over other kinds of traditional competitive games. For one, they attempt to involve all participants, unlike conventional games, which might select just a few gifted or experienced players. For these games, since there is no intention of having a winner or winning team, the emphasis on skills is minimized.

Eye Contact

Instruction

Formation: Participants are asked to "pair up" with one another. Typically, the group selects the person seated next to him or her. As the leader, it is often most efficient to assign pairs or partners. If there is an individual who does not have a partner, assign that individual the task of being an observer who will report to the group who has performed this task best.

Directions: The leader explains that this activity is used in a more serious context with salesmen and women to help them become more effective in their work. In our society, it is often considered awkward to look into another's eyes for a prolonged period. This activity is intended to overcome that uncomfortable feeling. The leader announces that participants must stare into the eyes of their partner for one and a half minute; they must keep their hands away from their faces, and not make funny faces, they should try to be serious. The result of this activity is quite amusing. Most participants cannot keep a straight face. They feel a bit self-conscious and discomfited while looking for ninety seconds into someone's eyes. When "time's up" is called, it is usually a relief. Participants are then asked to review how they felt. The individual who was an observer can now declare who had done this "the best."

One Hand Following Another

Free Play

Formation: This activity goes well with the preceding activity (Eye Contact) while participants are seated in pairs. They should be seated facing one another.

Directions: The leader asks participants to hold up their hands as they would to play pat-a-cake; that is, each individual will be looking at the backs of hands, thumbs side by side. The leader then says to place hands facing your partners—but do not touch. Once the leader sees everyone is in position he or she says that no further instructions will be given, but to simply have one hand follow another. This activity compared to the preceding one, Eye Contact, will be declared a lot more fun, lighter, and entertaining by the participants. It is much more pleasurable and congenial to do than staring into others' eyes. The two activities go well together.

Stress Exercise

Free Play

Formation: Ask all participants to stand. This works well if there is audience or classroom seating. Participants can stand in place, but ask them to spread out so that they are outside of arms reach. The title indicates they will be exercising which includes stretching. The leader will have had to practice this exercise in advance to ensure no mistakes are made.

Directions: The leader first asks that everyone raise their left arm—and follow him or her. This is done while the leader is facing the group and therefore raises his or her right arm. The leader then declares this as Move #1. Next, the leader asks that everyone hold out their left arm (horizontally), "this then is Move #2." The leader then puts his arm all the way down to his or her side and declares this as Move #3. Now ask that everyone repeat the same, and then label the succeeding Moves as #4, #5, and #6. Most participants will find this rather elementary. The leader nonetheless will ask that participants remember the Moves #1, #2, #3, #4, #5, and #6. Next, the leader asks that everyone raise their right arm—extended all the way. While participants raise their right arm, he or she raises her or his left arm. This move is declared as #1. Next, the leader asks that all participants lower their arm to their sides; this is labeled #2. The next move is to raise the stiffened arm all the way above their heads, and declare that as move #3; lower the arm to the side is #4 and raise it above heads, that's #5, and finally lower the extended arm all the way down to the sides to complete #6. Once again participants are asked to remember these moves. Now, all participants are asked to raise both arms together as the leader begins the count. Most participants are geared up for group exercise, however, what they soon realize is that this is not a common exercise. Once the leader begins calling #1, #2, #3, #4, #5, and #6, the group quickly becomes discombobulated, and breaks into laughter. The leader can then quickly ask that the participants pair up with one another, and face their partner, and then announce that the group will be asked to try it again. This makes for even more hilarity. Actually, some individuals are able to do this with ease and rather well!

Human Tangle
Free Play
Formation: All participants must join hands in a circle. The organizer then selects a leader in the group and asks that he or she releases the right hand.
Directions: The organizer announces that all participants must not let go of their hands, and instructs the leader to tangle the group by going as quickly as possible under the arms of the participants (who are holding their hands together). The organizer must repeatedly announce not to let go (of the hands), and must often prompt the leader to move more quickly so as to ensure everyone gets tangled. Once the group appears tangled, the organizer then asks the last person in the line to become the new leader and untangle the group. Most often, the new leader is given a lot of advice from the participants. Eventually, the entire group once again becomes an open circle. Sometimes facing out of the circle instead of facing the center of the circle. All participants are very impressed that they can actually get untangled.

Human Knot
Free Play
Formation: For this activity, eight participants per circle or group is ideal. If there are twelve persons, then divide the group accordingly so that there are six participants per group. The leader asks participants to join in a circle facing the center.
Directions: The leader demonstrates that all participants cross their arms, and when told to start, "Everyone walk toward the center of their circle and take the hand of someone, but not the person next to you." When everyone is asked to check to be sure he or she does not have the hand of the person next to him or her, the leader then tells the group, "Do not let go" and "Work your way out of the knot you are in." There is a lot of fun and humor that comes from this activity where people find themselves in an awkward position. Eventually, all participants open themselves up to a large circle still holding hands. In some rare cases, individuals will find themselves facing outward while others face inward.

Assassin/Killer

Free Play

Materials: slips of paper, pens/pencils, hat or bag

Formation: This activity is best with a minimum of 10 participants. This activity should be played by having participants sit in
a circle; another way that it could be done is to ask the participants
to mill around the room, continually walking. First, the leader must
ask everyone to write the last four digits of his or her telephone
number on a small slip of paper. (Another selection method should
be used if there is a chance that participants' phone numbers might
be known to others in the group.) The leader then collects the slips
of paper in a hat or bag and explains the following instructions.

Directions: The number chosen from the hat will be the person that
will be the assassin/killer. The way she or he will "kill" people is to
wink at them. The individual who receives the wink is "dead." He
or she cannot announce that he or she knows who the killer is. This
"dead person" simply puts his or her head down, and announces
"I'm dead." The object of this game is to find who the actual assas-
sin/killer is. The assassin/killer has to been very cunning, and be
careful not to be seen by the other group members. If an announce-
ment is made that a member believes he or she knows who the as-
sassin/killer is, and is wrong, then that participant is also dead. The
game continues until the actual assassin/killer is discovered. The
leader can then select a new assassin/killer by picking a new slip of
paper with a phone number on it.

Skin the Snake

Free Play

Formation: This activity works best outdoors on a lawn. However,
if conditions do not permit outdoor activity, the room must be
large enough for group members to lie down. To begin, players are
asked to stand in a straight line, alternating male and female, facing the back of the person in front. The leader must be very enthusiastic and assertive to see this activity through.

Directions: Once the group is lined up (with each individual facing the back of the other), the leader then asks them to place their
right hand between their knees. The next instruction is to "take
that hand (held between the knees) with your left hand." The
leader then makes the point that this is the snake. The first person
in the line (the snake's head) is then asked to move the snake forward—about four or five paces. Now, to "skin the snake," the last
individual in the line must lie down. It is important for the leader

to repeat the phrase "do not let go of the hands." This action (lying down) causes the entire line to move backward in this awkward position (hands held between legs). The next person in line is then asked to lie down between the legs of the person behind him or her; while this is happening the leader must remind all participants to not let go and to continue moving slowly backward. The leader should also ask the individuals lying down to hold their legs as closely together as possible. When all of the participants have laid down (between the legs of the person behind them, the leader can then say the snake skin has been removed, and skin the snake has been competed!

Dilemma and Resolution

Free Play

Materials: pens/pencils and paper

Formation: seated in a circle

Directions: Every other person is asked to take a 8.5 x 11 sheet of paper, fold it in half and then half again; now crease the paper on the folds and tear the sheets so that there are four slips of paper. The leader then asks that everyone in the group be certain to have two slips of paper. The leader then asks all participants to write a dilemma on one slip, such as "I went to the bathroom and there was no toilet tissue," and then on the other slip write the resolution or the decision made. Once everyone has completed writing, the leader then asks everyone to fold the slip with the dilemma and mark it with a "D." The leader then says, "please hold up the dilemma you've written in your right hand." This then will ensure there is full participation by all members of the group. The next command is, "now pass that slip two persons to your right." Once that is accomplished, the leader now asks everyone to fold the slip with the resolution, fold that slip and mark it with a letter "R." Now the leader asks the group to hold the slip marked "R" and pass it two persons to the left. This could be much fun unto itself—just passing these slips of paper. The leader asks first that no one open their slips until called on—to ensure spontaneity. Now, as might be expected he or she then selects an individual to begin and read the new dilemma they now have and then read his or her new resolution. This activity makes for much fun and hilarity as it uses surprise and spontaneity, coupled with chance, to create a dramatically different reading of the intended statements.

Projection

Free Play

Materials: pens/pencils and paper

Formation: seated in a circle

Directions: Prior to doing this activity, it is wise to have all participants recite their names so that everyone in the group knows each other's name. All participants are asked to sketch a certain object and not let the others see what it is he or she is drawing. Recommended drawings would be a sketch of someone in the room, including yourself; or another recommendation is for the leader to ask everyone to draw their own faces. The leader must emphasize that the entire sheet of paper must be used for the sketch—life size. A time limit is often necessary. Once everyone has completed their masterpiece, the leader then asks everyone involved to fold their artwork and the leader will then collect them. The leader now will hold up the artwork and ask the group to identify who that individual is. To add more interest and extend this activity, the leader may ask that individual to describe the portrait. Note: In lieu of drawing a face, the leader may direct the group to draw an experience or their favorite meal.

Fall Back and Pass on the Conveyor Belt

Competition

Formation: This activity is better to play outdoors. Each team is lined up facing one another, with arms held out in the imitation of a zipper. Arms stretched out toward the person they are facing do not touch or "lock." One participant from each team is asked to climb on a table or park bench and place his or her arms to the side.

Directions: This participant is then asked to face away from the line-up, place his or her arms and hands to their side, keep his or her knees stiffened and fall back pretending to be a log or a flat board. The leader then counts to three and says "timber." Once the "log" has fallen the team then passes the individual to the end of the line by jostling him or her so that they can move him or her to the back of the "conveyor belt" before the other team gets their member passed to the end. This activity can continue until all members of the group have been a "log" and passed to the end.

Chapter Eight
Music in Social Recreation Settings

Music is the language of the spirit; it is a universal means of communication and self-expression. All cultures in the world accept music as a highly desirable activity and usually hold talented performers in high regard. Music transmits emotions, such as sadness, love, fear, anger, pride, and patriotism. Music indeed contributes to one's cultural development and serves to contribute to a sense of personal adequacy. Music has been shown to strongly affect anxiety and depression in many individuals, particularly those with extraordinary cases. Music is considered a therapeutic modality by most physicians; it can change moods or feelings for individuals as well as groups. Everyone is endowed with some musical ability, which makes music especially useful for social recreation programming. Some basic components of music are melody, rhythm, verse or lyrics, and harmony.

There are two fundamental types of music program activities: community singing and musical games. Community singing usually consists of between 20 to 100 participants. Community singing is not just a trio or quartet of individuals performing together for fun. Since it does consist of a large number of participants, it does require assertive leadership and much enthusiasm on behalf of the leader. Perhaps a way to have a better perception of community singing is to look at it in the following context. Community singing is more common during the holiday season than other periods of the year, as many carolers join together at this time and can be seen in malls and shopping centers performing for a wide and varied number of audiences. Community singing is also carried out in halls, centers, and meeting rooms where Boy and Girl Scouts or volunteer, nonprofit agencies hold meetings.

To begin a community singing session, be certain that the singers are seated or standing close to one another. It is advisable to keep the sopranos, the altos, tenors, and basses together. Encourage singers to listen to each other. It is helpful to remind them that they are to sound as one voice, so that they may blend together.

Community singing is not easy to conduct. Most individuals of younger generations today have grown especially

shy when it comes to community singing. Not just anyone can
lead an enjoyable and successful sing-along. A leader of musical recreation programs does not have to be an excellent singer.
However, the leader should have a good sense of rhythm and
pitch, and, of course, be able to sing reasonably well for a
sustained period. The social recreation leader does not have to
read music, provided she or he knows the melodies fairly well.
Nor is it necessary for the social recreation leader to know conducting techniques. However, it is valuable to be able to make
simple gestures to help the group members sing in rhythm and
to give signals relating to dynamics, beginning and ending, and
other aspects of singing. Simple conducting techniques are to
move your hand and arm to indicate the music's meter. For example, one can conduct a musical piece in 4/4 time, by making
the hand and arm movement as though they were sketching a
square; each corner of the square then would represent a beat,
that is, 1, 2, 3, 4; 1, 2, 3, 4. To establish the pulse or beat for a
song in 3/4 time, one would move his or her hand and arm in
the shape of a triangle (e.g., 1, 2, 3; 1, 2 ,3).

Benefits of Community Singing

Despite its difficulty, there are enormous benefits and values
to providing community singing. One significant feature of
developing a community singing program is that the costs
for having such a program are quite inexpensive. Most of the
expenditures will be the result of making photocopies of the
songs for each of the members, and to further reduce costs, the
sheet music can be shared by two singers. Community singing
helps group members to relax with each other. This relaxation
comes about as a result of two reasons. One is because the fact
that participating individuals are taking deep breaths, inhaling
and exhaling, this then causes greater amounts of oxygen to
travel to their brains and this in turn helps relax the nervous
system. The other reason is because a feeling of camaraderie
develops soon after there is the sharing of a common goal, and
the long, soothing tones that emanate from each of the singers
helps to make the participants feel relaxed.

Community singing helps to break down the tension or
uneasiness that members of a new group often experience.
For established groups, community singing helps build group

spirit and unity. This type of singing is certainly recognized as a means of expressing human emotions. All age groups can do it. Community singing can also be very successful as an activity to be used by persons with various physical or mental disabilities.

Richard Kraus (1979, p. 99) identified the following six types of songs that are used or could be used in community singing:

1. *folk songs*, which include hymns and spirituals (e.g., "Kumbaya," "Amazing Grace") and songs of the pioneers (e.g., "Home on the Range," "The Ballad of Davy Crocket") as well as foreign songs that have become popular in the United States (e.g., "Guantanamera," "Allouette," "La Cucaracha")

2. *familiar old songs*, which are part of the American heritage (e.g., Broadway or movie musical hits), camp songs, and patriotic songs (e.g., "God Bless America")

3. *round and part songs* (e.g., "Row, Row, Row, Your Boat," "Frère Jacques") where the first group of individuals begins singing the first line of the song, and soon after they have begun, the next group of singers begin the same line of the song

4. *action songs*, which may actually resemble dances (e.g., "Hokey Pokey," "He's Got the Whole World in His Hands") where the leader directs the group to make the appropriate gestures to mimic the lyrics of the song

5. *dialogue and answer back songs* (e.g., "New York, New York")

6. *add-on songs* (e.g., "Old MacDonald Had a Farm," "The 12 Days of Christmas")

It is advantagous to begin song sessions with familiar songs that the singing group already knows. Do not begin with an entirely new piece. The interpretation for fast and slow songs is too broad, so what some might consider too fast, others might consider too slow. Therefore, do not be overly concerned whether the song has a fast beat or slow-beat.

Musical Games

Musical games, as compared to community singing, are far easier to conduct or lead. Following are several examples of musical games.

Scrambled Music Titles

Competition

Materials: prepared lists of song titles

Formation: At least two seated groups/teams. This can be accomplished by using the black and red cards of a deck of playing cards, or simply by asking the individuals seated in the center of the audience or class to move their chairs so that they would form two semicircles.

Directions: The leader will have prepared two sets of jumbled song titles. These titles should be of songs that are very well-known and popular. The song titles are written with a marker in a very large print so that they may be seen from the back of the room. The leader should have one to use as an example. The other selections of jumbled song titles, written on separate sheets, or 5 x 8 index cards, should number between eleven and twenty-one depending on the intended length of the activity. The leader would then place these titles on a table or chair and ask one person from the first competitive group to come up to hold the jumbled song title up to his or her chest for everyone to see. The first group/team to decipher what the correct title of the song is earns a point. The leader then asks a person from the opposing team to come before both groups and hold an index card of jumbled song titles. The first team to identify the song wins that point. Several individuals typically "jump the gun" and shout out their own song titles as they attempt to decipher the actual song title, and that makes for much hilarity. This activity works very well for shy persons as the leader only asks for minimal effort—that is, to hold an index card up before the audience or class. Suggested popular song titles are "The Star Spangled Banner," "She'll be Coming Round the Mountain," and "Moon River." To jumble these, move the letters in each word to a different position.

Name the Nation

Competition

Materials: pen or pencil and paper, prepared cassette tape or CD with melodies or pieces from a variety of countries or cultures. For example, the first piece might be a sample of American Indian music, the second piece could be from a country in Africa, the third from Turkey, etc.

Directions: This activity can be approached in five different ways (see Chapter Four, page 40 for details). If the first method is used, the leader plays the music and asks that the participants simply write down what they believe is the correct answer, or the leader might say, "from which culture or country is this music?" The response for this activity is particularly stimulating. It draws upon the multicultural aspects of our current U.S. urban societies, and provides participants with a bit of cultural education as well as much fun.

Name That Tune

Competition

Materials: prepared songs, cassette or CD player, pen or pencil and paper

Directions: There are five different ways to conduct this activity (see page 40). It is recommended that this sequence, or pattern be followed. For each of these different ways to play Name That Tune, the leader should have prepared a cassette or CD of different songs with which the group would be familiar. It is highly recommended that instrumentals, or instrumental sections be used rather than vocals. Ask the players to write down numbers 1 through 5 on their sheets. The odd number will help prevent ties in the game. You might like to extend the time for this way to play Name That Tune by asking players to write numbers 1 through 7 or 9. Explain that you will be playing a number of selections on a cassette or CD player for about seven seconds, and they are to write the title of the pieces—without revealing them to those seated near them. This is a popular game that also was once a television show. Its popularity is derived from the fact that nearly everyone shares this common denominator of listening to music. When participants are ready with their written answers, in this first way to play the game, the leader asks the group "Who has all the selections?" "Who has less than three selections?" The individual with all, or the most, titles to the selections, is the winner. To help balance out the competition level in multiple rounds, an important consideration at this time is to recognize this individual and be sure that he or she is later appropriately placed in a group that requires more assistance with identifying the melodies.

Guess The Christmas Song Title

Free Play or Competition

Materials: prepared list of popular holiday songs (see sample list below)

Formation: This can be done seated or standing. Of course, the leader must speak in a loud clear voice. This activity can either be done as an activity for the entire group, or the group can be divided into two or more teams.

Directions: The leader asks the group if they can determine the real title of the reworded Christmas song titles (answers on page 75). There is quite a bit of smiling, snickering, and laughter that occurs, during and after this activity, particularly when participants call out the wrong answers.

1. Noiseless Evening
2. Felicity Toward the Sphere
3. Adorn the Corridors by Means of Twigs With Red Berries
4. Saint Nicholas Is Traveling to the Borough
5. The Diminutive Percussion Lad
6. Self-Proclaimed Royal Trio
7. The Arrival of a Transparent 12:00 a.m.
8. Yonder in a Crib
9. The Deity Bids Relaxation to the Jolly Cultured Males
10. The Scarlet Proboscis Caribou Relative
11. Proceed Everyone Who Is a True Believer
12. Hollow Metal Spheres of a Shiny Precious Metallic Element From Which Pleasing Sounds Can Emanate When Shaken
13. From December to March—A Magic Place
14. The Initial Christmas Song
15. Icy the Homo Sapien of the Crystallized Water Vapor Variety

Answers

1. Silent Night
2. Joy to the World
3. Deck the Halls
4. Santa Claus is Coming to Town
5. The Little Drummer Boy
6. We Three Kings
7. It Came Upon a Midnight Clear
8. Away in a Manger
9. God Rest Ye Merry Gentlemen
10. Rudolph the Red-nosed Reindeer
11. O Come All Ye Faithful
12. Jingle Bells
13. Winter Wonderland
14. The First Noel
15. Frosty the Snowman

Chapter Nine
Square Dancing

Square dancing is a uniquely American type of dance. Many of the movements and steps have been borrowed or adapted from European countries such as Ireland, England, Germany, France, and Poland. However, this dance has its own character and appeal. It was a dance performed in the early history of America, when Puritanism and the Protestant Work Ethic meant little contact with the opposite sex. Square dancing is still quite popular today based on its lively music, festive mood, and its ability to create Flow for so many individuals who are appropriately challenged by the Square Dance Caller.

The benefits should be made clear to all participants. It should be apparent that dancing is a first-rate means of physical exercise and emotional release. Dance music provides rhythmic expression, allows individuals to express themselves in terms of rhythmic movements, develops muscular skills, and provides a mental challenge, especially for participants engaging in square dancing.

Square dancing must have a caller and appropriate square dance music. These days, it is easier to obtain a recording of the caller and the music than it is to actually hire live musicians. First, to organize the square dance, particularly for those who have never done it before, is to describe four basic steps: (a) the promenade, (b) circle left and right, (c) do-si-do, and (d) swing. If there are persons in the group who have done square dancing before, you may ask them to come before the group to demonstrate those steps. Aside from these basic steps, the leader should explain that the term *square* comes from the fact that nearly every room has a four walls, the "square" is represented in a "quadrille formation" also referred to as a "set." Each couple, made up of a male and female (when possible), joins in the center of room to form a circle of eight individuals. The couples are then asked to stand facing one another to resemble a square. The backs of the dancers are to the walls of the room. There are two "head couples" and two "side couples." The head couples are those who are closest to the caller; that is, the backs of one couple and the couple facing them and the caller are head couples. The other two couples are known as "side couples."

Indeed, this is a very highly desirable activity. Many "would be" participants may say they are not interested in dancing; however, once given the encouragement, or go-ahead, it is evident to all that these individuals clearly enjoy themselves enormously. Use one of the following mixers to help establish dance partners. The one that seems to draw out the most fun and humor is the Cinderella Mixer.

Cinderella Mixer

Free Play

Formation: Ask all the males to come to the front of the room. Once there, ask them to face the wall, and do not turn around. Ask the ladies in the room to sit in one line at the back of the room. If there is an imbalance between males and fe-males, then ask who would like to pose as the opposite gender for the sake of the dance. The leader will need a large plastic trash bag for this activity.

Directions: It is often necessary to remind the men that they are not to turn around; they must face the wall and not look behind them. When all the males are facing the wall, ask the ladies to take off both shoes and tell them they will not have to get up or walk (without their shoes). At this time, the leader collects both shoes from each lady, and puts only one in a plastic trash bag. The other shoe should be placed in a pile at one end of the line of seated ladies. Once all the shoes have been collected, the men are asked to turn and face the ladies. Everyone should then be reminded of the story of Cinderella, and how the prince searched for the woman who had lost her slipper. The leader then asks the first male to place his hand in the bag and select only one shoe without looking inside the bag. When this is accomplished, the first male finds the cor-rect owner of the shoe, the leader asks the next male to do the same. As the number of shoes diminish, the scheme picks up pace and all males should then have a partner with whom they can now engage in the square dance.

Matched Pairs

Free Play

Materials: The leader must prepare an appropriate number (according to the size of the group) of index cards with names of popular celebrities who have been known to have become a "pair" in history. Some examples of these are, Bonnie and Clyde, Ronald and Nancy, Cleopatra and Mark Anthony, Romeo and Juliet.

Directions: Separate the historic pairs into two piles—Distribute one stack to the men, and one to the women. Once distributed, the leader asks all participants to find who in the group is holding the match to the card he or she holds. Most often, there is much interaction and communication along with some humor, because some of the matches raise a comedic absurdity.

The Square Dance

Much of the leader's role in the dance is to first organize each quadrille formation, and review the basic dance steps (i.e., do-si-do, swing, promenade, and circle). The leader must be certain all participants have taken the appropriate formation. The leader should also divide the dance into sections after having listened earlier to the recording and noting the caller's commands to help prepare the dancers before the music starts. It is wise to review and practice the dance steps before the music is played. Two movements that typically begin the dance is to "honor your partner" and "honor your corner." This can be done by the traditional bow by the men; that is, one hand and arm placed in front and one behind. The ladies curtsy (if they are not wearing dresses, then they would just go through the motions) before their partners and corners.

Once a review of the four basic dance steps is completed, and all participants are in place, the music can begin and the dancers would follow the caller.

Chapter Ten
Dramatic Games

In social recreation programs, dramatic activities are quite informal. They are less structured than regular acting performances that most of us are familiar with, in that they are conducted with a minimum of preparation or rehearsal. Most of us commonly recognize the training, talent, and professionalism that goes into theater, Broadway, or off-Broadway performances. Informal dramatic activities are those which do not require special talent or exceptional acting skills; in nearly all cases, they do not require memorization of lines and waiting for cues. Some examples of informal dramatics include, but are not limited to, blackouts (where there is no proper curtain to change scenes, instead lights are just turned off), shadow plays, pantomime, charades, storytelling, skits, dramatic games (e.g., games using drama), and script-in-hand (where it is much more advantageous to have the participants write their own).

In social recreation the idea is to have group fun; in this case, there is much fun to be had on a number of levels. First, for the leader, there are few instances when it is necessary to have many props or supplies; the leader may very well ask participants to bring a pen (or pencil) and some paper on which to write. Secondly, these informal dramatic activities help individuals learn to work together and to value each other's contribution as they often have to wait, or rely on others before speaking or doing their part; it is clear that much cooperation is necessary. Thirdly, these activities can be used with a wide variety of age groups: older, mature participants can, without doubt, participate in the informal drama along with very young participants. Fourth, persons who are shy or withdrawn (which is true for so many youth today) can feel free to loosen-up and behave in a fashion they would not otherwise feel is appropriate. Lastly, a true value in providing informal dramatics is that these activities allow participants to engage in various forms of expression. Before beginning the activity session on informal dramatics, it is advisable to begin with asking the group to demonstrate the sort of dramatic expressions they, themselves could act out "here in this room." Some typical forms of expression, they may offer include happiness, sadness, confusion, tiredness, romance, surprise, and anger. While voluntary comments are being offered by participants, the leader should ask all participants to observe the individual who could display or act out the expression offered or stated.

Fashions in Paris

Free Play or Competition
Materials: two sets of newspapers, two rolls of scotch tape, paper and pens/pencils
Formation: This could be in done with each group in opposite corners of the room.
Directions: The leader asks the two groups to select a male model for each group. This model will be dressed in the latest fashion—made of newspaper. Each group is to select a song they will sing while the model presents himself in front of both groups. The leader must ask that one person from each group be the announcer and prepare a written statement about this new fashion (which will be read aloud)—Items such as the ticket price for this outfit, a description of its detail, including color, design, perhaps major headlines, and so forth, like a fashion show. The leader must emphasize a time limit to prepare the model, the song, and the introduction. It is best to announce to both groups the remaining time. While the groups prepare the models, the leader should arrange an aisle for the model to walk down. This could be done using chairs lined up. When the two groups are ready, the leader asks the first group to present their model. The model walks down the aisle as the group sings their entrance song, and immediately after that the commentator reads his or her statement about the fashion.

If You Love Me, Please Smile

Free Play
Formation: This activity requires at least twelve participants. All participants are asked to form a circle while standing.
Directions: Ask the group to recall the expressions they identified earlier (typically they are happiness, love, sadness, anger, confusion, and surprise). They are to use these acting expressions when performing this activity. The leader must make it clear that there are two lines to be memorized to do well in the dramatic activity: (a) "Darling, I love you. If you love me, please smile," and (b) "Darling, I love you, but I cannot smile." The leader then selects the person to stand in the center of the

circle and chose any individual to make the first statement. The first participant selects an individual in the circle and tries his or her acting skills on him or her: "Darling, I love you, if you love me, please smile." Since the return message has to be, "Darling I love you, but I cannot smile," typically, that individual cannot keep a straight face, and breaks into laughter, which then snowballs into more hilarity with the entire group.

Skit in A Bag

Free Play or Competition

Materials: plastic trash bag for each team filled with articles of clothing, including hats, and objects (e.g., a Frisbee)

Formation: It is always best to use names rather than ask the group to "count-off" numbers. For example, the leader may designate the two teams by saying "one team will be from Mary to Ed, and the other team will be from Bill to Jane." Both teams should get the same sort of items.

Directions: The leader must set a time limit for this activity. He or she directs the groups to prepare a short skit (e.g., play) that includes each member of their team. The results are fascinating and demonstrate the unique creativity of groups that are given the same (or similar) objects, but produce quite different skit outcomes.

Storytelling Challenge

Competition or Entertainment

Formation: Form two seated groups.

Directions: Name four or five random items (e.g., desk, car, rug, flower) and ask the participants to use their imaginations and storytelling skills to devise a story. This can be used as a contest or a competitive game to have the entire group determine which group actor has done the best job.

Contest Using Letters of the Alphabet

Competition or Entertainment

Materials: paper and pens/pencils, chalkboard

Directions: Ask the group to state which emotions can be acted in this room by these group members. A list should be written, either on paper or preferably on a writing board or chalkboard of all cited emotions (typical choices are anger, sadness, romantic love, happiness). Two individuals are asked to come before the seated audience and stand back to back.

When the signal is given, the two contestants are told to face the audience and starting with the first emotion listed on the board, begin using only letters of the alphabet to act out the emotions given by the group. The two contestants speak their arbitrarily chosen letters simultaneously, and both try to use vocal inflections in such a way as to make it clear which emotion is being conveyed, expressed, or acted out. For instance, shouting "A!...B!...C!" etc., perhaps using clenched fists and an exaggerated scowl, would work well for an emotion such as anger; or using other letters such as R, W, or Y to emote sadness. This informal dramatic activity could be conducted as an actual contest with the selection of a winner by the audience. The leader would ask the audience who they believe actually did the best job. Many times there will be such hilarity that the two contestants will be complimented for their efforts automatically and a "tie" declared.

Team Charades

Competition

Formation: Review the rules of Charades (i.e., the player/actor must not speak or write what it is he or she is attempting to communicate); the group should say anything that comes to mind (not just sit and be a spectator) as this might trigger another, more accurate response. The player/actor can use long-established gestures (e.g., "sounds like" by pulling on his or her ear lobe, the number of syllables by tapping on his or her arm, using his or her fingers to indicate the word he or she is trying to get his team to say is the second or third word in the title). This activity requires at least two teams. The teams are seated apart from one another so that the opposing teams cannot hear each others' discussion.

Directions: Each team is asked to write, on three individual slips of paper, the title to (a) a movie, (b) a book, and (c) a TV show. Once both teams have done this, one team member from Team A is asked to come before the two groups and without speaking communicate to his or her group the title on the slip of paper. The leader should restate that the members of the team should say whatever comes to mind as that might trigger another team member's correct response. As the team member faces his group to try to communicate the title of the movie, book or TV show, she or he is carefully watched by the opposing group. The opposing group, of course knows the title, since they had just discussed it.

Chapter Eleven
Party Planning

Essentially, there are two types of parties: theme parties and holi-day parties. Theme parties have a topic or idea built into the entire event. Examples of these theme parties would be a Hawaiian Luau, a retirement party with artifacts from the workplace as memora-bilia, a Valentine's Day party, or a St. Patrick's Day party.

Planning a Party: Procedures and Guidelines

Generate Interest and Awareness

First and foremost is to generate interest among the intended guests. Before actually going further with detailed plans, it is wise to be certain there is enough interest and enthusiasm among the group members. Do not allow yourself to be the only eager indi-vidual to plan all aspects of the party—as this can be a "road to disaster."

Have a Theme

Most parties in which there are more than twenty-five participants have a reason for the celebration. This purpose should be carried out in terms of a theme. For example, a Valentine's Day party would have red hearts and cupids for the decorations, and the in-vitations could have poetry or phrases that relate to romance and love. Perhaps the drinks would be in red cups or contain red soda or juice. Possibly popular romantic love songs would be played as guests enter. The point is to be sure to carry out the theme of the party.

Create a Festive Ambiance

When the event begins, there are many ways to create a festive feeling and party atmosphere. First would be to use decorations, in keeping with the theme, such as balloons and hanging cutouts from the ceiling. A distinctive floral bouquet or an ice sculpture might be used as a centerpiece. Candles might also be set on tables to offer a certain warmth. It is advisable to have nametags made for the guests, particularly if they are not well-acquainted. It is also an excellent idea to have either the host or hostess greet the guests as they arrive, and welcome them as they enter.

The Order of Events

Probably the most difficult aspect of party planning is to know when to introduce specific activities. The sequence of which activity comes first and which comes next can change with each situation. By their nature, all parties are not alike. Thus, it is very important to plan the timing of each episode of the party. Here too, Maslow's Hierarchy of Human Needs (see Chapter One, page 7) can be helpful. There appears to be a natural flow of events that established itself as the appropriate method to use when hosting a party.

For all concerned the room with its decorations, lighting, and seating arrangement should allow the guests to feel safe and secure. Traditionally, guests expect to have refreshments initially and something to eat. Once this has been satisfied, people are usually drawn to conversation in small groups. When this is well-established, they then enjoy having some form of entertainment. At this point, it is a very good idea to make use of the entertainment activities offered in Chapter Six, as well as to have ready at least two mixers or ice-breakers to begin the party. A major distinction between a typical party and a successful party is the typical party has refreshments, conversation, and perhaps some background music. A successful party has a number of activities in which all participants can share in the joy and celebration. An appropriate selection of activities, allows participants to loosen up and not feel shy. The right choice of activities, when designed correctly, can make the party a truly memorable one. This will have been, as Maslow might say, an event in which nearly all participants had an outstanding time together and left with a feeling of having fulfilled their expectations (resembling self-actualization).

Evaluate

One of the major distinctions in this approach to party planning is the idea of reviewing and rating not only the entire party itself—once completed—but the components that led to its success or failure. Evaluation is making a determination as to what went well and what aspects of the event should be repeated in a way that will allow the group to create the same winning sensation. Of course, on the other hand, a fair review of the party will examine the negative components as well and have those components eliminated for the next time that same event/party is to be planned. If something was done particularly well, as was indicated by (a) the compliments and comments received from the participants and (b) the fact that the majority of participants remained until the designated concluding or closing time (or time to go), that would be a positive sign that the party planning went well and that nearly everyone had a enjoyable experience.

Party Preparation Components

The major components to the successful party include invitations, decorations, refreshments, and program activities. Note that while the first three are commonly found in the typical party, the dissimilarity here is that unlike typical parties, social recreation parties have program activities. Program activities make the difference between a typical party and a successful party.

Typical Parties Versus Successful Parties

While it may appear that the parties discussed herein are those that can be conducted in private homes, the original intent is to use this information for planning parties for professional recreation agencies described earlier in this book; that is, this information is chiefly intended for use in Boys and Girls Clubs, YMCAs, YMHAs, Boys and Girls Scouts, Senior Citizen Clubs and Community Recreation settings. This does not mean that this information could not be applied to personal house parties; it can be—although it may very well have to be adjusted.

When planning a typical party at home, one individual usually takes control and does all the planning. This is not advisable for recreation professionals who are to plan a party for a large group of perhaps, thirty to a hundred. Instead, once the date and time is established for the party, it is strongly recommended that the recreation professional engage at least two to four individuals to plan and carry out the tasks. To attempt to carry out all the tasks alone would be extremely difficult and inevitably lead to mistakes, errors, and an unpleasant experience for the leader and the guests as well. In the typical party, which normally has fewer than twenty-nine guests, the usual pattern is to establish a guest list, decorations, a menu, which would include hors d'oeuvres, beverages, entrees, and desserts, the table seating, and preparations initially when sending the invitations, and again the week before, the day before and the day itself. A successful party does have all these but the most important difference is that the successful party has social recreation program activities.

Holiday Parties

A general list of holiday parties would include New Year's Day, Christmas and Chanukah, Easter, and Independence Day. Parties are also often conducted on Valentine's Day, St. Patrick's Day, and Halloween. Indeed, each of these has a theme built into them to assist in being recognized and distinguished as special days in the year to which people look forward.

Review Questions (short answer, multiple choice, True or False (T or F)

1. What is the most popular use of free time today?
2. Does TV encourage a spectator-oriented approach to leisure?
3. What is discretionary time?
4. Has there been a decline in the influence of social institutions (e.g., the church, the family) in establishing predetermined roles for individuals?
5. Has there been an increase in physical fatigue associated with many forms of employment?
6. What is the name of the ethic on which the U.S. value system is established?
7. How do most members of today's society tend to regard their recreation and leisure: highly valued or of only marginal worth?
8. How many general ways (or categories) are there to present social recreation activities?
9. How many levels of participation are there? What are they?
10. Does a social recreation leader constantly tell others what to do?
11. What blocks creativity?
12. An important part of the definition of fun is spontaneity. T or F?
13. The intentions of this book include the following: encouraging readers/students to develop an appropriate attitude towards leisure, develop/practice group interaction skills, and develop a repertoire of activities. T or F?
14. A good example of a social recreation activity is a pet show. T or F?
15. Objectives of social recreation include athletic competition. T or F?
16. What does FORCE stand for?
17. Is social recreation chiefly intended for small groups (less than thirty)?
18. Who was Abraham Maslow?
19. Public recreation and parks department offer instructional classes and free play sessions for children. T or F?
20. Employee recreation programs offer wellness and stress reduction programs. T or F?

Set #2

1. Our Armed Forces provide MWR (morale, welfare, recreation), and the emphasis is on diversion, relaxation and morale. T or F?

2. Puritan work ethic represents the concept of being antileisure and antirecreation. T or F?

3. Outdoor recreation includes camping and nature activities. T or F?

4. A major reason for the growth of recreation is modern technology. T or F?

5. Correctional recreation means leisure activities for inmates. T or F?

6. Recreation therapists work with persons with disabilities. T or F?

7. A 4-H Club is referred to as a voluntary youth organization. T or F?

8. The highly specialized nature of employment in this age of automation has a tendency to remove us from close social relationships found in the work of our forefathers. T or F?

9. Are longer work hours a reason for the growth of the recreation profession?

10. What is discretionary spending?

11. To ensure the most effective social recreation program, it is essential to repeat a pattern of presenting one activity in the same identical form each day the group meets. T or F?

12. The decline of the influence of social institutions, such as the church and the family, in establishing predetermined roles for individuals in all aspects of life, has affected social recreation participation. T or F?

13. Physical fatigue, associated with employment, has resulted in _____ pursuit of leisure and recreation. (a) increased (b) decreased

14. During much of our history in the United States, our value system was heavily influenced by the work ethic. T or F?

15. What does marginal worth mean?

16. Put the life stages in the order described by Eric Erickson.

17. Is competition in social recreation games and other activities the main purpose of participation?

18. The unique value of social recreation is its stress on formal participation and individuality. T or F?

19. Do movies, television, electronic toys, or games do as much as social recreation to promote human dignity, self-worth, and help individuals develop social skills?

20. As a student of social recreation, do you believe you must travel great distances and buy expensive equipment to find pleasure?

Set #3

1. Do all business and governmental organizations in the world sponsor social recreation programs?

2. Is community recreation supported by grants, members' donations, and/or fees?

3. Is a carnival a program activity?

4. Is it a goal of social recreation to provide cultural enrichment?

5. Younger children should be age _____ to enter more formal recreation programs. (a) 4 (b) 10 (c) 3 (d) 12 (e) 8.

6. A program for employees that is least likely to be classified as social recreation is a (a) cruise (b) banquet (c) Christmas party (d) combative sports event (e) chartered travel vacation

7. A major emphasis in this book is (a) habit and conformity are necessary for fun (b) leaders do not serve as role models (c) individuals must find their own way (d) to sit quietly and observe (e) to develop constructive group relationships

8. We learned from which activity to not make assumptions and read more carefully? (a) the Stirrers Trick (b) 3 and 5 Gallon Containers (c) Apples and Oranges (d) the Aptitude Test (e) the Personality Test?

9. An important element in the definition of fun is: (a) it must always be humorous and jolly (b) everybody should have a good time (c) spontaneity (d) good drinks (e) happiness everywhere

10. Is the role of the leader affected by his or her professional peers?

11. Does a good social recreation leader develop a system of recognition for all participants?

12. Can a social recreation event take place anytime, anywhere, with any number?

13. Is it a function of a social recreation program leader to be a counselor?

14. Is it a function of the social recreation leader to approve policies and set goals?

15. Is the role of the leader affected by the attitude of the group?

16. Does the composition of group members have a major affect on the recreation leader?

17. Does recreation always reduces stress?

18. Is it a function of a social recreation program leader to be a disciplinarian?

19. What leadership theory describes the belief that you see the group's needs and desires and therefore become leader?

20. What leadership theory describes the charismatic leader?

Set #4

1. What leadership theory says the circumstances determine who becomes leader?

2. Which leadership theory says that a leader's success is based on characteristics of the group and the difficulty of tasks?

3. Is providing for happiness anywhere included in the list of social recreation objectives?

4. How large should the size of a group be for maximum interaction to occur and for the leader to be able to relate closely to each person?

5. What is sociometrics/sociometry?

6. Does a competent social recreation leader demand that every participant do his or her best at all times?

7. What is one of the best ways to reduce stress, especially for those who have high tension levels?

8. What was the most difficult aspect of doing the Couples String Trick?

9. The activity "Ad Phrases" uses competitive teams. T or F?

10. What is the minimum number of participants necessary for conducting "Levitation"?

11. Recreation is more closely associated with social psychology than with sports. T or F?

12. Recreation is a combination of the characteristics of work and play. T or F?

13. Which of the three leadership styles is the most preferable in social recreation?

14. With children, a couple of years difference in age will greatly affect the skill level, interest, and social abilities of their participation. T or F?

15. What are the two specific types of parties?

16. Which Pattern of Leadership says the leader accepts the decision of the group?

17. Which Pattern of Leadership allows for members to make individual appeals?

18. Which Pattern of Leadership describes the assertive leader?

19. Which Pattern of Leadership says the group accepts leaders advice?

Set #5

1. Which Pattern of Leadership says the leader is "feeling out" the group, or asking them?

2. What are the steps to "how to lead games" in a proper order?

3. Are festivals program activities or special events?

4. Are social recreation activities found in nurseries?

5. Do all leaders have to become charismatic?

6. Do government and businesses sponsor low organized social recreation programs?

7. Are organizations that are not professional recreation agencies likely to provide social recreation events?

8. Have games only recently been used to transmit social values?

9. Who wrote *Games People Play?*

10. A special value of social recreation program activities is its emphasis on informality and leadership. T or F?

11. In what sort of group would you find more satisfaction and cohesiveness?

12. Is group dynamics a professional area of study centered in social psychology?

13. What is a confederate or shill?

14. A group that is open and has a changing membership is _____ tolerant? (a) *more* (b) *less*

15. Who is more likely to take risks and try new activities, women or men?

16. How many times should you, as a social recreation leader, ask individual group members to participate?

17. Is shared leadership an important objective of social recreation?

18. Maslow became popular because of his studies about motivation. T or F?

19. Is group dynamics concerned with developing techniques for effective group management?

Set #6

1. Good Social Recreation programs are a result of careful planning. T or F?

2. The most efficient way to make two groups is to join hands in a circle. T or F?

3. Remember Scrambled Music Titles? Was it in the competition category?

4. In social recreation and seated in a competitive circle game, should you keep players in the circle and give them a point if they get the answer wrong, or should you take them out of the circle?

5. *New Games* emphasize noncompetitive activities. T or F?

6. Can just anyone lead a community sing-along?

7. What are blackouts?

8. What are rounds?

9. *Social Recreation: A Group Dynamics Approach* by Richard Kraus is an outstanding resource for activities.

10. In social recreation games, it is often advisable to organize the larger group into competing groups. T or F?

11. What are the five guidelines to party planning?

12. What are the major goals of social recreation?

13. What are some examples of social recreation activities that fall under the category of competition?

14. Is Overtake under the category of competition?

15. Under what category is Name That Tune?

16. Under what category is the Couples String Trick?

17. Is a cooking club the same as an activity of a continuing social group?

18. New Games fall under the human potential movement. T or F?

19. What are Growth Games?

20. Once this book is completely read, can the reader really be expected to lead with these activities?

Answers to Review Questions

Set #1

1. Watching television

2. Yes

3. Free time, time not spent at work

4. Yes

5. No. Most jobs in these last three decades are not as physically demanding as jobs in the past.

6. The Puritan (or Protestant) Work Ethic

7. Most members of today's society tend to have a very high regard for their personal recreation and leisure.

8. There are four categories for presenting social recreation activities: instruction, demonstration, competition, and free play.

9. There are three levels of participation: program activities, special events, and clubs or activities of continuing social groups.

10. No. Unlike some art forms or the military, which can be very demanding, social recreation does not have one leader continuously telling others what to do.

11. Blocks to creativity include lack of knowledge, lack of energy, and aspects of fear, habit, and conformity.

12. True. While it may be difficult for a group to agree on what constitutes fun, it will always be agreed that spontaneity makes a condition, situation, or event fun.

13. True. It is necessary to have a minimum of at least three activities ready when presenting in a social recreation setting. Presenting one activity might be adequate, but it is best to plan on turning to something new and different when the situation calls for it.

14. True

15. False. Social recreation represents what a group can do to have fun aside from sports and athletics. In most cases, social recreation emphasizes cooperation and not competition.

16. FORCE stands for Familiar Ordinary Relaxed Casual Experience, which is the essence of social recreation

17. Yes. To go beyond twenty-five persons in a group is very difficult, beyond thirty persons is extremely difficult. Social recreation is chiefly intended for small groups between six and twenty-five.

18. Abraham Maslow was a psychologist who wrote about the hierarchy of human needs.

19. True

20. True

Set #2

1. True

2. True

3. True

4. True

5. True

6. True

7. True

8. True

9. No. Work hours of the majority of today's society have been cut to an average of 37.5 hours.

10. Discretionary spending refers to money that you can spend at your own will. This is usually money available after paying for basic necessities, rent, utilities, transportation costs, and other bills.

11. False. It is important to have novelty and spontaneity built into program planning.

12. True

13. (a) increased

14. True

15. Marginal worth means of little value. Some persons in our society feel that recreation and leisure activities are of marginal worth.

16. The stages of life that affect social recreation most are: (a) young children (b) adolescents (c) young adults, (d) middle-aged adults and (e) older adults

17. No. They are not the main purpose, although competition may be used to enhance activities.

18. False. Social recreation stresses informal participation and group identity.

19. No. Especially for younger persons who are developing physical, emotional, cognitive and social skills, social recreation can provide socially approved means of having fun with one's peers.

20. Social recreation has great potential for assisting in the development of new friendships and enhancing older friendships. The real pleasure in life is not necessarily where you go in this world, it is the people you're with.

Set #3

1. No. Not all business and government agencies sponsor social recreation programs.

2. Yes

3. A carnival is not a program activity—It is a special event. Usually a carnival occurs very rarely, perhaps once a year.

4. Yes. Social recreation provides numerous opportunities to meet and mingle with others while engaging in activities that involve music, dance, drama, and the expression of one's ethnic heritage.

5. Children should be (e) age 8.

6. The answer is (d) combative sports event. This type of event is usually boxing, a wrestling match, martial arts, or can be extended to include football.

7. (e) This is one of the major goals of social recreation.

8. (d) There are several statements in the Aptitude Test where people just assume they know the answer.

9. The answer is (c) spontaneity.

10. Yes, very much so.

11. Yes. It is judicious and advantageous for the augmentation of group cohesion.

12. No.

13. Yes. It is not uncommon for social recreation leaders to act as counselors when individuals in the group have personal difficulties.

14. Yes

15. Yes

16. Yes

17. No, it does not. Social recreation is not a panacea for distress.

18. Yes

19. The functional theory of leadership

20. The trait theory

Set #4

1. The situational theory
2. The contingency theory
3. No.
4. Between ten and twelve persons
5. Sociometry is a study of the level of interaction within a group, and sociometrics can help to determine who might be a potential leader of the group, and who is withdrawing from interaction with the group members.
6. No
7. Physical exercise or physical activity
8. Of utmost difficulty is to keep the attention of all group members and to have them partake in the fun.
9. True
10. The minimum number is eight. There are five people involved in the demonstration; there should be at least three persons to serve as an audience.
11. True
12. True
13. The democratic style is most preferable.
14. True
15. Theme and holiday
16. Joining
17. Consulting
18. Telling
19. Selling

Set #5

1. Testing
2. (a) Prepare yourself and the necessary materials; (b) motivate the group; (c) explain the point of the activity; (d) take formation (e.g., circle, sitting, standing, line, audience seating, table seating, couples); (e) demonstrate and explain; (f) practice or walk-through the activity; (g) conduct the activity, play the game, perform the dance, etc. (h) end the activity or game by using a signal or advanced notice.
3. Festivals are special events

4. No

5. No. That is impossible.

6. No. Most often they do not enjoy playing simple games.

7. Yes

8. No. Games and toys have been used for centuries to transmit social values

9. Eric Berne wrote *Games People Play*.

10. True

11. More satisfaction and cohesiveness would be found in a homogeneous group with few members

12. Yes

13. A confederate (or shill) is a decoy—someone who is planted in the group by the leader to pass signals to him or her.

14. More tolerant

15. Men

16. You should ask potential participants at least three times, in different ways of course.

17. Yes

18. True. He developed the hierarchy of human needs.

19. Yes.

Set #6

1. True

2. True

3. Yes. Scrambled Music Titles is a competitive game

4. A major point: Keep them together (in the circle) and do not reject them from the circle.

5. True

6. No, not just anyone. The leader of a community sing-along must have a good sense of pitch, a strong voice, and a sense of rhythm aside from knowing the melodies to be sung.

7. Blackouts are used on drama stages where a curtain is not used to change the scene.

8. Rounds are songs sung by groups where the second line of people in the group repeat the same exact phrase as the preceding line of people just sang.

9. True. This is an excellent resource for social recreation activities.

10. True

11. The five guidelines to party planning are (a) arouse interest, (b) carry out the theme, (c) create atmosphere, (d) plan program sequences, and (e) evaluate.

12. The major goals of social recreation are to develop constructive group relationships, to develop and enhance old friendships, to develop group morale and cohesion, to provide experiences in democratic living, to identify with others and enjoy the accompanying sense of belonging, to develop a sense of personal worth, to provide opportunities for emotional release and relaxation, to strengthen one's value of leisure, to provide cultural enrichment, and assist in the development of leadership

13. Name Bingo, The Friendship Mixer, Ad Phrases

14. Yes. Overtake is under the category of competition.

15. Competition

16. Entertainment or Demonstration

17. Yes. This is one of the Three Levels of Participation.

18. True

19. Growth games are more serious in their intent than are New Games, which are both innovative group games. Growth Games are to assist participants in developing self-knowledge, self-awareness, self-expression and self-acceptance.

20. Yes. The activities in this book were selected because they are not too difficult to lead.

Resources

American Camping Association

5000 State Road 67 North
Martinville, IN 46151
Phone 765-342-8456
Fax 765-342-2065
http://www.acacamps.org

Games Publications, Inc.

P.O. Box 203
Marion, OH 43305-0203
Phone 800-426-3768

Kendall/Hunt Publishing Co.

4050 Westmark Drive
P.O. Box 1840
Dubuque, IA 52004-1840
Phone 800-228-0810
Fax 800-772-9165
http://www.kendallhunt.com

National Recreation and Parks Association

22377 Belmont Ridge Road
Ashburn, VA 20148
Phone 703-858-0784
Fax 703-858-0794
http://www.nrpa.org

Venture Publishing, Inc.

1999 Cato Avenue
State College, PA 16801-3238
Phone 814-234-4561
Fax 814-234-1651
http://www.venturepublish.com

Bibliography

Allen, R. and Beattie, R. (1984). The role of leisure as an indicator of overall satisfaction with community life. *Journal of Leisure Research, 16*(2), 99–109.

Cain, J. and Joliff, B. (1998). *Teamwork and teamplay*. Dubuque, IA: Kendall Hunt.

Csikszentmihalyi, M. (1997). *Finding flow: The psychology of engagement with everyday life*. New York, NY: Basic Books.

Diener, E. (2000). Subjective well-being: The science of happiness and a proposal for a national index. *American Psychologist, 55*(1), 34–43.

Frank, R. (1999). *Luxury fever: Why money fails to satisfy in an era of excess*. New York, NY: Free Press.

Godbey, G. (2003). *Leisure in your life* (6th ed., pp. 80–81). State College, PA: Venture Publishing, Inc.

Harris Ericson, J. and Albright, D. R. (1996). *File o' fun* (3rd ed.). State College, PA: Venture Publishing, Inc.

Jackson, E. L. (1990). Variations in the desire to begin a leisure activity: Evidence of antecedent constraints? *Journal of Leisure Research, 22*, 55–70.

Jackson, R. and Schmacher, S. (1997). *Special events inside and out*. Champaign, IL: Sagamore Publishing.

Johnson, D. and Johnson, F. (1997). *Joining together: Group theory and group skills*. Needham Heights, MA: Allyn & Bacon.

Kay, T. and Jackson, G. (1991). Leisure despite constraint: The impact of leisure constraints on leisure participation. *Journal of Leisure Research, 23*(4), 301–313.

Krane, G. (1998). *Simple fun for busy people—333 free ways to enjoy your loved ones more in the time you have*. Berkeley, CA: Conari Press.

Kraus, R. (1979). *Social recreation: A group dynamics approach*. St. Louis, MO: C.V. Mosby Co.

McLean, D. D., Hurd, A. R., and Rogers, N. B. (2005). *Kraus' recreation and leisure in modern society* (7th ed., pp. 112, 136). Sudbury, MA: Jones and Bartlett Publishers.

Michaelis, B. (1991). Fantasy, play, creativity and mental health. In T. Goodale and P. Witt (Eds.), *Recreation and leisure: Issues in an era of change* (3rd ed., pp. 55–72). State College, PA: Venture Publishing, Inc.

Michaelis, B. and O'Connell, J. M. (2004). *The Game and play leader's handbook* (Rev. ed). State College, PA: Venture Publishing, Inc.

Myers, D. and Diener, E. (1997, September). The science of happiness. *The Futurist, 31.*

Nelson, P. (2000). An aging population: The challenges and the opportunities. *Journal of Family and Consumer Sciences, 92*(2), 10–11.

Powers, P. (1991). *The activity gourmet.* State College, PA: Venture Publishing, Inc.

Tangley, L. (2000, June). Aging brains need fresh challenges to stay agile. *U.S. News and World Report,* 90.

Yankelovich, D. (1982, May). The work ethic is underemployed. *Psychology Today, 6.*

Index

About the Author

John V. Valentine, Ed.D., is an associate professor in the Department of Physical Education, Recreation, and Health at Kean University in Union, NJ where he has been teaching since 1980. He has much experience in the specialized format of the recreation profession identified as social recreation. He was voted Teacher of the Year by Kean University's Alumni Association, and he is a long standing board member of the Boys and Girls Clubs of Union County. He is the author of several articles about the importance and value of activities in group settings. His appreciation for recreation activities is associated with his love for music, as he is also an accomplished ethnic-folk musician and lecturer.